What **BRAIN RESEARCH**

Can Teach About

CUTTING SCHOOL BUDGETS

To Lillian Warneke
(January 18, 1921–December 5, 2008)
If we're lucky, we meet a teacher who takes an interest in us and furthers us along.
If we're even luckier, we meet a teacher who helps us choose our path in life.
If we're very, very lucky, we meet a teacher who blazes multiple paths for us—
paths leading to a life that would not have been even remotely possible
without the broad and deep range
of knowledge and skills he/she taught us.
In a small, rural high school offering a seven-period day
for fewer than 60 students, to which I traveled 50 miles,
Lillian was my teacher for English III, IV, composition, senior civics,
speech, drama, choral music,
and life.
Writing and speaking, classes that were excruciatingly difficult
for a painfully shy student,
have been the cornerstones of my professional career.
Her view of the purpose of government fueled my drive
to contribute to the world,
and music has been a love and joy without which I could not have survived.
To the Lillian Warnekes everywhere,
thank you for being our teachers
and helping us make more of our lives than we could have ever dreamed.

What BRAIN RESEARCH Can Teach About CUTTING SCHOOL BUDGETS

Karen D. Olsen
Foreword by Susan Kovalik

CORWIN
A SAGE Company

For information:

Corwin
A SAGE Company
2455 Teller Road
Thousand Oaks, California 91320
(800) 233-9936
Fax: (800) 417-2466
www.corwin.com

SAGE India Pvt. Ltd.
B 1/I 1 Mohan Cooperative
    Industrial Area
Mathura Road, New Delhi 110 044
India

SAGE Ltd.
1 Oliver's Yard
55 City Road
London EC1Y 1SP
United Kingdom

SAGE Asia-Pacific Pte. Ltd.
33 Pekin Street #02-01
Far East Square
Singapore 048763

Printed in the United States of America

Library of Congress Cataloging-in-Publication Data

Olsen, Karen (Karen D.)
What brain research can teach about cutting school budgets/Karen D. Olsen.
    p. cm.
Includes bibliographical references and index.
ISBN 978-1-4129-8049-4 (pbk.)
    1. School budgets—United States. 2. Education, Elementary—United States—Finance. 3. Brain—Research. I. Title.

LB2830.2.O57 2010
371.2'06—dc22   2009037011

This book is printed on acid-free paper.

10   11   12   13   14   10   9   8   7   6   5   4   3   2   1

Acquisitions Editor:	Hudson Perigo
Associate Editor:	Julie McNall
Editorial Assistant:	Brett Ory
Production Editor:	Cassandra Margaret Seibel
Copy Editor:	Jeannette K. McCoy
Typesetter:	C&M Digitals (P) Ltd.
Proofreader:	Scott Oney
Indexer:	Jean Casalegno
Cover Designer:	Rose Storey
Graphic Designer:	Karine Hovsepian

Contents

Foreword

Susan Kovalik

Because the making of a historical benchmark isn't readily identifiable while it is being framed, it takes courage and insight to see possibilities and act upon them. During the past 30 years, neuroscience has handed us one benchmark after another—a wealth of information on the human brain and its functions, giving us opportunities to increase learning in ways not previously possible.

New technologies have allowed us to peer further and further into the mysteries of the human brain. And although we certainly don't yet know all we'd like to know, we certainly know enough to enrich the learning of our students and the knowledge base of our teachers. The brain research used in this book is as solid as it comes—and its applications tested in thousands of classrooms. This is happening, as Robert Sylwester says, "on our watch," and we should hold ourselves responsible for using this information as the compass by which we make decisions regarding what happens in our schools.

With tough financial times upon us, we need to work smarter, not harder. The ultimate significance of this landmark book is that it foreshadows a not-so-distant future in which all decisions in our public schools will be based upon principles from brain research, not on tradition, or "the way we do things here," or upon philosophies of education endlessly debated. The clear, succinct, no-nonsense descriptions of brain research findings in these pages will become the bedrock for decisions involving hiring, planning, funding, implementing, and assessing what we do in our schools.

Author and coauthor of more than a dozen, theory-to-practical-application books over the past 25 years, Karen D. Olsen is uniquely suited to the job of expanding our awareness of the practical, and powerful, uses of solid concepts from brain research. This book, her latest, represents a bold step forward in making practical use of brain research by offering a guide for decision making when cutting school budgets.

Karen's first large-scale project was using brain science to improve science education using the Kovalik ITI model (now known as *HET—Highly Effective Teaching*) with its strong brain research base. This was a 10-year, $3 million effort funded by the David and Lucile Packard Foundation. More than 500 teachers in five counties participated in the Mid-California Science Improvement Program (MCSIP), each for a minimum of three years.

As Executive Director of the MCSIP program, Karen was deeply involved in the day-to-day work of the participating teachers and, as a result, wrote several key books—*Kid's Eye View of Science: A Teacher's Handbook for Implementing an Integrated Thematic Approach to Science, K–6* (coauthored with Susan Kovalik), *Classroom Stages of Implementation*, and *Science Continuum of Concepts, K–6*—all aimed at helping teachers move from theory to practical application of neuroscience.

The brain research findings briefly described in this book were well tested during the MCSIP project (1987–1996) and have since been expanded and deepened through the work of dozens of trainers, associates of Susan Kovalik & Associates, working with thousands of teachers throughout the United States, Canada, Europe, Japan, and Indonesia.

This book will be considered a historical benchmark, causing all stakeholders involved in school budgeting to look with new eyes on what truly advances learning in their schools. It's not about how much money our schools have; it's about how that money is spent.

This book is also a useful guide when adding new funding, such as stimulus money and post-recession expansion funds, or when merely wanting to spend money more effectively.

Preface

Too often, the process of budget cutting leaves wounds that take years to heal; idealism withers, hope for a better program dies. In the face of serious challenges, positions harden and philosophies of education become both sword and shield. From this cauldron emerges a book that offers a means of dispassionate, rational decision making based on principles from brain research.

Although the idea of applying brain research to the budget-cutting process may startle, using brain research to improve schools has been around for more than a quarter of a century. The brain research base used in this book is especially well documented. The brainchild of Susan Kovalik & Associates, the ITI model (now referred to as *HET—Highly Effective Teaching*) has developed over the past 25 years based on the experiences of thousands of teachers in countywide, districtwide, schoolwide, team, and individual teacher implementation environments. The model was one of 22 chosen for inclusion in the Comprehensive School Reform Program effort in 1999 and was also selected by Dr. Charles M. Reigeluth, Indiana University, as one of only a handful of models that met his stringent criteria for a curriculum-instruction model (see *Instructional-Design Theories and Models, Volume II: A New Paradigm of Instructional Theory*, edited by Charles M. Reigeluth, Indiana University; also see *Exceeding Expectations: A User's Guide to Implementing Brain Research in the Classroom*, 4th ed., by Susan J. Kovalik and Karen D. Olsen). The outcomes of this brain-based model—improvement in student achievement and personal and social growth—are predictable and well documented.

Given this track record, the author's assumption that brain research can help us with the very difficult process of cutting school budgets is neither pie in the sky nor a "bridge too far." As the reader will soon discover, the very principles from brain research that have helped schools improve their program and student outcomes are precisely the same principles that can be used to analyze where money and time (and time is money) are ineffectively spent and thus can be cut with minimal harm.

The book revolves around the Strategy-Builder Chart in Chapter 1 that identifies where dollars might best be cut, rated on a scale of 1 to 10. This helps stakeholders formulate a game plan—what to take on, when, and in what order.

But cutting one's budget is only part of story. A basic premise of this book is that simply cutting budget—and suffering through with what's left—is a poor strategy. The author insists that we must *cut more than enough* so that there is money that can be reinvested in those areas that would significantly improve student outcomes—and lift the spirits of staff and parents. Thus, the second part of the Strategy-Builder Chart is a 1–10 rating scale of where small amounts of money can be reinvested to greatest effect.

Chapters 2 through 10 provide a road map for analyzing and making decisions in the areas of instructional tools, organization, and use of time, staffing, professional development, movement, emotion, curriculum, and testing.

Each chapter provides the following:

- Action Items—specific steps that will help you think through how to analyze your program for budget-cutting potential and how (and when) to reinvest some of the money. These action items also include tips on group process strategies. Where appropriate, there are separate discussions for those in self-contained environments (usually elementary school) and for those in departmentalized situations (typically middle and high school).

- Brain Research—brief summaries of brain research relevant to the decision making needed to cut your budget and to reallocate some monies to the areas most likely to increase student achievement with little cost.

- Resources—in addition to recommendations for further study, there are more than 30 analytical charts to aid in gathering needed information.

- Endnotes—comments on references identified in the footnotes to give the reader a perspective on the resources mentioned and help with deciding if a book or article should be shared with stakeholders now or in future planning. Also included are anecdotal stories to illustrate important ideas and help participants connect information to their own experiences.

- Action Summary Checklist—a summary of all of the Action Items outlined in the chapter.

Budget cutting is a painfully personal process. Throughout this book, the author has chosen to use the first-person voice—to talk in terms of you and me and us. The choice is a deliberate one, chosen because budget cutting is all too often attempted in the third-person "remote" voice—as if the lives of real people aren't being disrupted. But the truth is, when it comes to budget cutting, very real people must make very real decisions that affect very real people and students. So, there is nothing to be gained by attempting to seem impersonal or cloaked in the anonymity of bureaucracy. To do so lacks courage and is dishonest.

A very difficult job awaits. This book is intended to light the way and lighten the load.

Acknowledgments

No book coalesces from thin air. It bears the traces of the hands and minds that touch it. This book is no exception. Friend and colleague Sue Pearson provided invaluable feedback and editorial support, chapter by chapter. With blistering speed and amazing patience and gentleness, she prodded and queried, making this a better book than I could have hoped for. I am indebted to her expertise, wisdom, and good cheer.

Thanks also to Olga De Santa Anna, principal of Mintie White Elementary, Watsonville, California, and Linda Jordan, Professor, Hope College, Holland, Michigan, for giving me encouragement halfway through the project when I needed it most, assuring me that there was both need and desire for a book such as this.

Thanks also to the colleagues who were willing to take a moment out of their busy schedules to read the prepublication draft of this book with a practitioner's eye and provide valued feedback:

Terri Patterson—Director, Elementary Education, Waco Public Schools, TX

Patty Harrington—trainer, ITI/*HET* model, CA

Denise White—ITI/*HET* practitioner, middle school, Thoreau Academy, Tulsa, OK, and ITI/*HET* trainer

Barbara Norris—K–6 ITI/*HET* practitioner, Brevard Public Schools, FL, now retired, and ITI/*HET* trainer

And to my writing partner, Mr. Pum, who never failed to sense when the pressure was mounting and I needed a good purr to get me back on track, thank you for sharing the past decade of keyboard loneliness so peculiar to authors. I shall miss your soft footprints across my desk and your propensity to nap on the very pages I was working on.

PUBLISHER'S ACKNOWLEDGMENTS

Corwin gratefully acknowledges the contributions of the following reviewers:

Laurie Emery, Principal, Old Vail Middle School, Vail, AZ

Richard Jones, Principal, John Adams Middle School, Rochester, MN

Lynn Kaszynski, Principal, Harrison Street Elementary School, Sunbury, OH

Michelle Kelly, Teacher, Great Falls Public Schools, Great Falls, MT

Beth Madison, Principal, George Middle School, Portland, OR

Amanda Mayeaux, Associate Principal, Donaldsonville High School, Geismar, LA

Mark Merrell, Principal, James Madison High School, Vienna, VA

Lyndon Oswald, Principal, Sandcreek Middle School, Ammon, ID

Introduction

Those who liken cutting a school budget to traversing a minefield may be dismissed as melodramatic, but they err on the side of realism. The task challenges on every front: group process skills and strategies, creating common ground and a shared vision from which to work, finding the time to build community, building morale rather than losing hope, requesting waivers for unworkable federal, state, and local requirements, and handling individual fears about change in position or even genuine fear of losing one's job. The list goes on. And the current economic downturn suggests that schools will be living this budget-cutting scenario for some years to come.

To succeed, we must change our thinking. We must build on new information—solid, validated concepts about how the human brain learns, new conceptualizations about how schools can be structured to best focus on student needs instead of bureaucratic convenience and inertia. Most of all, we must make budget cutting a part of program improvement so that all decisions are made within a larger picture of who and what we want to be.

As you begin this book, study Chapter 1 carefully. Your beginning point, and ongoing touchstone, is the Strategy-Builder Chart. Let the author's 25 years of moving brain research theory to practice help you develop a realistic and effective game plan. Study the chart. The largest money pools that can help you meet your budget-cutting requirements—and stay consistent with brain research principles—are in the areas of instructional tools and testing. Be prepared to request waivers of some requirements. Saving money in the area of staff is usually accomplished through attrition and better organization and use of staff time.

The most cost-effective areas—meaning those in which you can expect the most improvement in student outcomes for the least reinvestment—are the areas of movement and aerobic exercise (a big surprise for most of us), organization and use of time (common sense), and professional development (no surprise). Where to reinvest is a matter of strategizing, not merely prioritizing; some of our biggest problems are simply too costly to address during a time of shrinking funds. Strategizing requires that we be open to new methods to achieve an old goal or to giving up an old goal for a better one.

As the three possible game plan scenarios in Chapter 1 suggest, there are many ways to skin the cat. Choose a scenario that you can succeed with from day one and that will also lead you into the future.

1

Where to $tart

No one in his right mind wakes up one morning and says, "Yessss! Today I get to cut my school's budget!" With or without stimulus money, the day of serious budget cutting is here, and in every school across the country. The challenge is how to do so and end up with a better program in the process. And how should we spend that stimulus money? Hopefully, it can be spent to stimulate long-lasting improvements without creating a need for ongoing expenditures. It all starts here.

ATTITUDE IS IMPORTANT

When adversity strikes, attitude is important. We can either count ourselves as victims of circumstances beyond our control and waste time grieving and being angry over our plight or we can commit ourselves to making the most of the situation. When cutting budgets, and especially when leading the process, it is essential that we take the high road and make sure that the changes inherent in budget cutting go in the right direction—toward program improvement.

Throughout our short history as a nation, necessity has always been the mother of invention, the driver of learning that leads to new solutions. The tidal wave of inventions during the Westward Movement, World War II, going to the moon, and

> *"There is nothing wrong with change, if it is in the right direction."*
>
> —Winston Churchill

developing the personal computer are good examples of American ingenuity when called upon. And in public education, are there problems to fix! Until the current economic crisis is resolved and America finds its economic footing in the 21st century, we are likely to be asked to cut our budgets by as much as 35%.

Emotional Versus Dispassionate Decision Making

The mere hint of the need to cut the budget, or even failing to expand funding to move forward, is a serious morale buster. And understandably so. But if we are to succeed at our task, we must immediately take steps to ensure that emotions won't hijack our ability to think clearly.[1]

To shift the playing field, two elements are essential: community building and group process.

Community Building[2]

To make and live with the decisions needed to cut your budget requires the following:

- Building a sense of community—in which the sense of belonging drives a desire to work toward the common good
- Creating common ground—in which everyone is empowered to speak and all listen with respect; this creates the basis for influence that matters and influence that works for the common good
- Taking action—commitment to be an active participant in decision making and the integrity to implement the decisions made by the group(s) responsible for making the decisions (whether or not we were a member of that particular committee)

> *"Never doubt that a small group of thoughtful, committed citizens can change the world; indeed, it is the only thing that ever has."*
>
> —Margaret Mead

A sense of community doesn't just happen. It requires initial work and day-by-day monitoring and reinforcing. There are countless books on this subject, a topic well beyond the scope of this book. However, one of the resources specifically designed for school communities, one with a 30-year track record, is the TRIBES work and training by Jeanne Gibbs. (See *Reaching All by Creating TRIBES Learning Communities*. Windsor, CA: CenterSource Systems, 2006.)[3]

Another effective training for school communities is the restitution social development work of Diane Gossen. (See *Creating the Conditions: Leadership for Quality Schools* by Diane Gossen and Judy Anderson. Chapel Hill, NC: New View Publications, 1995.)[4]

Whatever training program you choose, do it. And stick with it. The work you do here will make or break all that you do.

Group Process

Planning how a group will work together has at least three goals:

- Nurturing community building
- Getting the group through the work at hand in the most effective and efficient way possible
- Building understanding of the decisions reached and raising commitment to implement them

Leading groups through high-emotion, high-stakes work requires skill and believable neutrality. This is also a field filled with thousands of books and hundreds of models. My favorite model, because of its power and simplicity, is that developed by Bruce Tuckman in 1965. The forming, storming, norming, and performing stages of group development, according to Tuckman,[5] are all necessary and inevitable for the team to grow, face up to challenges, tackle problems, find solutions, plan work, and deliver results. Each has its demands on the group facilitator—agenda planning, facilitating the meeting, and follow-up.

An effective group facilitator is a must. Either look for someone in the community who is willing to donate his or her time or provide facilitator training for a staff member who is respected as an effective listener.

An important element in group process is establishing and sticking to ground rules such as the following:

Ground Rule 1: After sincere acknowledgment of the emotions,[6] establish a "no whining" rule. As our mothers used to say, "If you don't have something nice (in this case, constructive) to say, don't say anything."

Establish an agreed-upon hand signal for group members to use to remind the person speaking that he or she is slipping into whining. Stay positive. Negativity will kill the group and stymie your efforts.

Ground Rule 2: No looking back. Conduct a formal burial ceremony. For example, have each participant write on a small piece of paper what upsets him or her most. Set a paper-shredder on a table in the middle of the group and ask each person to "let it go" for good as he or she runs the memento through shredder. Or if an outdoor ceremony is preferred, place the paper slips in a paper bag and bury it or burn it. Make an agreement to move on together.

Ground Rule 3: Avoid the easy way out. Don't accept simple solutions that were created for earlier situations (which thus might make them seem more acceptable). To end up with a better program, a straightforward, unflinching approach must be taken. Of course, it won't be easy. But it's doable.

ACTION ITEMS

Action Item A: Gather a leadership team[7] and set ground rules

"Start by doing what's necessary; then do what's possible. Suddenly, you are doing the impossible."

—St. Francis of Assisi

If you don't already have one, form a collaborative leadership team to serve as a steering committee as quickly as you can. Include the principal, vice principal(s), teachers, other certificated and classified staff, parents, and, at secondary levels, students. The membership of this team should be considered a good representation of the stakeholders at your school. Set the tone and the ground rules for schoolwide discussions.

Determine how to best acknowledge the disappointment, frustration, and anger that program disruption and change will engender. Then, quickly move on to productive discussions about *what to keep, what to cut,* and *what will be needed* to make what's left work well, even better than before. Keep the vision that this new program can be even better than before.

Ground rules for working together are essential to the decision-making process.

Establish ground rules for your leadership team and post them in the room each time your group meets. Briefly remind the group of them as you start to work.

Action Item B: Clarify the purpose

Clearly establish who must be protected during budget cutting. Students and the quality of their learning environment must be the first and primary criteria for all decisions.[8]

Admittedly, this will be a difficult principle to hold to. However, Mr. Spock (of *Star Trek* fame) was right: *The needs of the many outweigh the needs of the few.* Recognize that protecting jobs, rigidly holding to last-in, first-out rules, and other such traditions must be set aside. If budget cutting is the necessity and a better program is the goal, all decisions must be based on what is best for *students.*

Appoint a recorder to write down all agreements—policy and procedural. Record in a PowerPoint or Word file that can be forwarded to each group member immediately after the meeting. Begin every subsequent meeting with a review of these agreements (on screen or printed out). Rotate the recorder duties for each meeting.

Action Item C: Have a game plan

A basic premise of this book is that simply cutting budget—and suffering through with what's left—is a poor strategy. We must *cut more than enough* so that there is money that can be reinvested in those areas that would significantly improve student outcomes—and lift the spirits of staff and parents.

The best game plan begins with a commitment to improve programs—using reallocation of some resources after budget cutting as a means to get you there. Use the Strategy-Builder Chart in Figure 1A to help plan your strategy—where to start and where to go, step by step. To create such a game plan, two questions must be answered:

> Simply cutting budget and suffering through with what's left is a poor strategy.

- Where to cut? Identify the biggest sources of funds that can be cut, especially those expenditures that aren't consistent with brain research.
- Where should we reinvest? Identify areas with a high cost-efficient ratio—a few reinvestment dollars will produce the biggest achievement increases.

The chart (see Figure 1A) answers those questions.[9]

The *first column—"Source of $ to Cut"*—rates the size of funds available for cutting (10 is high).

The *second column—"Cost-Efficiency Ratio"*—indicates the potential cost-efficiency ratio when reinvesting funds; in other words, where can a little bit of money buy a significant increase in student achievement (10 is high).

Strategy-Builder Chart

Program Area	Source of $ to Cut	Cost-Efficiency Ratio—High Achievement Increase for Low Cost
Instruction		
Tools (textbooks, worksheets, Internet, reference books) (Ch. 2)	10	7
Organization and use of time (Ch. 3)	3	8
Staffing (Ch. 4)	8	6
Professional Development (Ch. 5)	1	9
Bodybrain Partnership		
Movement and aerobic exercise (Ch. 6)	0	10
Emotion (Ch. 7)	1	9
Curriculum		
Content for Link One (Ch. 8)	2	7
Content for Link Two (Ch. 9)	0	9
Testing (Ch. 10)	10	3

Figure 1A

How to Read the Strategy-Builder Chart—Examples

A. There are three areas with high potential for budget cutting—instructional tools (for example, textbooks, workbooks, and copy machine plus paper and time to create worksheets), staffing (through attrition), and testing.

B. The most cost-efficient areas in which to reinvest are movement and aerobic exercise, professional development, organization and use of time, and emotion.

C. Although there is likely no money that can be cut from professional development, professional development has a high cost-efficiency ratio for reinvesting.

D. There is likely little money that can be cut from organization and use of time, but a great deal can be done without reinvesting any money—change that will remain within current resources from year to year.

Some of these improvement areas, such as organization and use of time and initiating a movement program, are relatively inexpensive and can be fully implemented within weeks. Others, particularly developing curriculum to fit the Two-Step Learning process (see Chapters 8 and 9), will take much longer and require considerable inservice training over time; however, if they are to be implemented, first steps should begin as soon as possible. All actions must be prioritized carefully so they will fit within your diminishing resources.

Remember, there is no one best place to start nor one best path. Begin where it makes the most sense for your school, set a path through the issues that work for your stakeholders, and travel at a pace that will add sanity to an otherwise turbulent time.

> *"Delay is the deadliest form of denial."*
>
> —Northcote Parkinson

See the game plan scenarios discussed on pages 1.9 through 1.11.

Action Item D: Remember—This is a time of national economic crisis and urgency for students

Be honest and realistic without being alarmist. Continuing business as usual is a guaranteed recipe for disaster in your school. Free yourselves to be creative—think outside the box. Commit yourselves to the proposition that there are no sacred cows; everything and every penny must be open to scrutiny and analysis. This should include the portion of categorical monies that have been allocated for district office expenses, maintenance and repairs of buildings and grounds, and ongoing janitorial services as well as classroom expenses . . . everything.

This is also a time of urgency on behalf of students. We simply MUST find more effective, and cost-efficient, ways to improve learning for *all* students.

Invite a parent artist to draw a picture of a brain sitting outside a smaller box and another picture of a sacred cow with a prohibited sign (red circle with diagonal line, traffic sign style). Post these in the room every time your group meets; use them as humorous reminders to the group to think outside of the box and to never compromise for the sake of a sacred cow.

Action Item E: Shift the thinking

Recognize that Einstein was right: "Today's problems cannot be solved by the thinking that created them." Before starting your discussions about what to cut, realize that you're at the start of a steep learning curve. To make the best decisions, you need new information. And more important, everyone must be willing to let go of old assumptions, old paradigms, and old practices.

This is not a time to hold tight to what has been; this is a time to be *bold*, to be willing to turn adversity into opportunity. Acknowledge the fact that this will not be easy. Recognize that previous accomplishments may get pulled apart in the process. Come to grips with the reality that budget cutting cannot be avoided.

And what is this new information that is needed? It's information that will help you remain dispassionate in your decision making, information that will help eliminate those unresolvable debates over differing philosophies of education—debates that have the same effect as filibustering in the U.S. Senate . . . impasse, death by ideology. The best idea should be the winner, not the person with the strongest social position.

What's needed is information about research into how the human brain learns and how to use it as a template for dispassionate decision making. At the first (no later than the second) meeting of your group, assign each member a brain research section (found in Chapters 2–10) to read. Using the jigsaw collaborative process, have each member share his or her key points with the group.

Action Item F: Stay in the "here and now"

Get into and *stay* in a "here and now" mode of thinking. This is critical on many levels. First, "the way it's always been done" mode excludes newer staff and parents from being able to fully participate, making their time-limited observations seem less valid. If anything, in a budget-cutting process, history is an impediment. You must make your decisions based on what is before you right now. Yesteryear's solution may have become today's problem (or part of it) or less effective due to staff turnover and lack of training for newcomers. A fresh perspective from someone with no vested interests is invaluable.

Second, base your decisions on actual current effectiveness, not on theoretical impact or prior results. For example, in theory, lowering class size should increase student outcomes, but it does so *only if*

- Instructional strategies and materials change to take advantage of the instructional opportunities available when teaching fewer students (the same instructional strategies and materials that aren't very effective with 30–35 students aren't effective with 20 students either)

and

- The adults in the room are well trained and proficient in how to use those tools and processes.

The same is true of efforts to reduce the student-adult ratio within a classroom.

"What could be or should be if" is a ruinous pitfall.

To help shift your perspective, visit other schools[10] that have moved in the directions you want to go.

Action Item G: Involve others

Once your leadership team has its feet on the ground, begin to involve others, eventually including the entire staff and interested parents and community members. Have an "each one bring one" day at least once a month. Because everyone must live with the decisions to be made, it is essential that everyone understand why the decisions were made and respect the process that produced them. Even if someone doesn't agree with a decision, your school community can survive, and even thrive, *if*—and this is a very big *if*—there is respect for the process as well as for the principles chosen to guide the decision making.

Keep repeating these words: transparency and openness, transparency and openness . . . principles versus personalities, principles versus personalities.

Action Item H: Provide the necessary time

Give the gift of time. Remember, frequent, short meetings are much more effective than a few long ones. Much has to happen between meetings. People need time to adapt to the need for change, to learn, to reflect, to grow, to become a team member assigned to a difficult task, to choose to take responsibility for difficult decisions, to change one's mind and go public about it, and to become a leader for cutting budget and improving program.

Start today. Set a schedule that shows commitment to this process and one that is backed by sufficient resources to ensure your success. Be sure your agenda for each meeting is clear and the process for moving group members from item to item has been well planned in advance.

Action Item I: Anticipate parent response

Every parent knows his or her child has but one chance at kindergarten, one crack at fourth grade, and so forth. With that in mind, it is not unreasonable for parents to fear change at their child's school. How detrimental to their child will the loss of the abandoned things be? Will the new approaches be implemented well enough to be successful in the first year?

Such fears are neither surprising nor unfounded. Most people prefer the known, even if dissatisfied with it, to the unknown. New doesn't necessarily mean better. A superb idea inadequately implemented will be no more beneficial than what it replaced.

For each program area outlined in subsequent chapters, *create a parent committee* to advise you on parent concerns—a marketing research group to alert you to concerns and the kinds of information parents will need to understand the reason for the changes and how best to communicate that information to parents and community.

Assign a staff member to meet with this parent group. Listen closely to what they have to say. Put yourself in their shoes; pretend you are the parent and it is your child who needs his or her best shot at grade-level _____ (fill in the blank).

Avoid educational jargon; make it understandable. Keep focused on what's best for students. Use parents' native language whenever possible to ensure that information is clearly explained and accurately understood, and that questions get answered.

RESOURCES

Mapping out a strategy that is doable within the time available and the conditions within which you must begin your work is fundamental to your success. As you consider the Strategy-Builder Chart on page 1.5, consider several alternatives, and then pick the one that will give you the greatest success now and each year thereafter.

Possible Game Plan Scenarios

As mentioned before, there is no one best way to tackle budget cutting and program improvement. However, the following will give you a starting point for developing a game plan that best fits your circumstances.

Game Plan Scenario 1

This book falls into your hands after January, making planning time very short. Consider limiting the scope of your work to these steps for the year:

Step 1: Start with Chapter 2: Instruction—Tools.

- Complete Action Items A through E and J through K. Allow replacement of consumables for key textbook adoption series only on a teacher-by-teacher basis. Invite teachers whose students always do well in the subject area to be creative.

- Divide the money you've saved into categories:
  - Money needed to meet budget-cutting requirements
  - Money to be reinvested in movement and aerobic exercise and professional development
- Return to your analysis of tools in spring, summer, or early fall as time allows.

Step 2: Read Chapter 4: Staffing.

- Complete Action Items A through E. Analyze the positions that will come open due to attrition. Refill only those positions that are urgently needed for student safety or positions that are a keystone in a heavily funded program that must continue.
- Divide the money you've saved into categories:
  - Money needed to meet budget-cutting requirements
  - Money to be reinvested in movement and aerobic exercise and inservice
- Return to your analysis of staffing in late summer or early fall when openings are known for sure. Again, refill only those positions that are urgently needed for student safety or are keystone positions.
- Address Action Item F the day school begins in the fall.

Step 3: Read Chapter 6: The Inseparable Bodybrain Learning Partnership—Movement and Aerobic Exercise.

- Complete every Action Item in this chapter. Make this your only focus for program improvement for next year. Reinvest sufficiently in this area to fully implement your plan in one year. Include in your plan how new hires will be brought fully up to speed. The impact of a fully implemented movement and aerobic exercise program will produce impressive improvements in student achievement that will ease community fears regarding additional budget cuts and reinvestments. This will make future work much easier.

Game Plan Scenario 2

This book falls into your hands at the beginning of the school year, but the prior year's budget-cutting process left behind unhealed wounds and distrust of the process.

Step 1: Carry out Steps 1 through 3 described under Scenario 1.

- Pay particular attention to group process as you do so.
- Recommendation: Bring in a consultant to advise and assist you with relationship building, group building, and group process. If possible, recruit a parent or involved community member. Key criteria: an effective listener, one capable of putting his or her own agenda or point of view aside to be truly neutral.

Step 2: Read Chapter 10: Testing.

- Complete Action Items A through G.
- Obtain district, state, and/or federal waivers to cancel or reduce testing for next year.
- Be aware that completing the planning and implementation you'd like to accomplish in this area will take time, probably two to three years. Plan and implement accordingly.
- Divide the money you've saved into categories:
  - ○ Money needed to meet budget-cutting requirements
  - ○ Money to be reinvested

Game Plan Scenario 3

This book falls into your hands at the beginning of the school year, and your staff and school community are prepared to address the challenge of budget cutting and are looking forward to the opportunity to improve the program for students in the process.

- Tackle this book in its entirety.
- Consider addressing the chapters in the following order:
  - ○ Phase 1: Chapters 1, 2, 4, and 6 and the initial cutting of funds in Chapter 10 plus the necessary Professional Development
  - ○ Phase 2: Chapters 3 and 7 plus the necessary Professional Development
  - ○ Phase 3: Chapters 8 and 9 and the necessary Professional Development and completion of Chapter 10

ENDNOTES

1. The power of emotions to hijack the cerebral cortex and disrupt analytical thinking is a well-researched area of brain research. For a brief tour of these phenomena, see *Exceeding Expectations: A User's Guide to Implementing Brain Research in the Classroom,* 4th ed., by Susan J. Kovalik and Karen D. Olsen (Federal Way, WA: The Center for Effective Learning, 2009).

2. These stages of community building come from the *HET* model. See *Exceeding Expectations,* vol. 2: 9.2–6.

3. The TRIBES training that accompanies this book is available through CenterSource Systems: 1-707-838-1061; fax, 1-707-838-1062.

4. Group training that accompanies this book is available through Chelsom Consultants. See RealRestitution.com.

5. Tuckman created a fifth stage, adjourning and transforming, to cover the end of a project and the breakup of the team. Unless marked by some kind of celebratory event to publicly encapsulate the successes and fond memories of the experience, the breakup can become a phase of mourning. Given the number of tasks to be performed during a time of budget cutting and a finite number of players, it is important to pay attention to this phase so that members enter the work of the next committee with a feeling of pride and accomplishment as well as

confidence that the new committee experience will also end positively. See Tuckman, "Developmental Sequence in Small Groups," *Psychological Bulletin,* 63, no. 6 (1965): 384–399. See also www.mph.ufl.edu/events/seminar/Tuckman1965 DevelopmentalSequence.pdf. A good resource for Tuckman and other group building resources is www.teambuilding.co.uk/.

6. Ken Blanchard and Margaret McBride, *The One-Minute Apology: A Powerful Way to Make Things Better* (New York: William Morrow, 2003). Blanchard's other one-minute books also have valuable tips for working within organizations as well as managing oneself.

7. What leadership teams should be established and who should be on them will vary depending on the political climate of one's school and district. Clearly, the wider and more inclusive and genuine the involvement, the greater the buy-in to the decisions made. District office and board members must also be involved as they must become allies in changing district policy and procedure. This is not a time for business as usual. All must be involved in rethinking what we do and how we do it.

8. This is *not* to suggest the goal of budget cutting should be to eliminate jobs but rather to assert that what each employee does should be best crafted to improve learning experiences for students. Also, if any vacancies occur, do not automatically refill them. Monies from such salaries can become the resources needed to meet your budget-cutting goals and to improve your program.

9. The ratings in the Strategy-Builder Chart in Figure 1A are based on the author's observation of program improvement efforts over the past 20 years that used the ITI (now referred to as *HET—Highly Effective Teaching*) model, a comprehensive model of curriculum and instruction based in brain research.

10. Susan Kovalik & Associates has been training schools in how to implement brain research in the classroom and schoolwide for 25 years. See their Web site at www.thecenter4learning.com.

ACTION SUMMARY CHECKLIST

_____ Action Item A: Gather a leadership team and set ground rules.

_____ Action Item B: Clarify the purpose.

_____ Action Item C: Have a game plan—Remember, simply cutting budget and suffering through with what's left is a poor strategy. Use the Strategy-Builder Chart in Figure 1A. Choose or adapt a game plan scenario for your circumstances.

_____ Action Item D: Remember—This is a time of national economic crisis and urgency for students.

_____ Action Item E: Shift the thinking.

_____ Action Item F: Stay in the "here and now."

_____ Action Item G: Involve others.

_____ Action Item H: Provide the necessary time.

_____ Action Item I: Anticipate parent response.

2

Instruction—Tools

I n every profession—be it carpentry, farm-ing, data processing—tools matter. They set the ceiling for excellence that can be achieved and the efficiency and cost-effectiveness by which that excellence can be attained. Teaching is no different.

> $ Cutting Potential—10
>
> Cost-Efficiency Ratio—7

How we teach matters. And the how is directly determined by the tools available to us and those required of us. While the push of tradition to use textbooks, workbooks, worksheets, and the ubiquitous ditto is for-midable, brain research couldn't be more clear or definitive about the innate deficits of such instructional tools.

A BRIEF SUMMARY

In a nutshell, *learning is the result of real physiological growth in the brain that occurs due to massive sensory input.* We have 19 senses, not five,[1] and

- the more senses that are activated, the greater the stimulus to the brain; and
- the greater the stimulus to the brain, the greater the likelihood that learning will occur and be wired into long-term memory.[2]

There are no shortcuts to be taken here. All outside-the-body informa-tion comes to the brain via the sensory system. When sensory input is rich, the brain grows. When sensory input is weak or limited, physiological change in the brain is unlikely.

See the back of this chapter, beginning on page 2.8, for a brief look at brain research in this area. Also, consult your own learning experiences, those of your own children, and your own observations of your students over the years. This research will not surprise you, but it definitely challenges the status quo, including the beliefs about instructional tools entombed in No Child Left Behind.

ACTION ITEMS

These action items are a beginning point. Resources for carrying out each step can be found at the end of the chapter.

Action Item A: Establish the membership

Establish the membership of the work group responsible for analyzing instructional tools. (Note: The steering committee established in Chapter 1 is a likely group to establish the membership of this group and to oversee its work. If possible, include all teachers at each grade level to carry out this task. Willingness to implement often hinges on the depth of understanding of the why and how behind the what. It also increases commitment to the team effort.)

Set your meeting calendar. Survey your members to determine what information they might need to fully participate in this process. Be especially aware of the information needs of parents, community stakeholders, and classified staff members.

Action Item B: Analyze your instructional tools

After studying the Brain Research section at the back of this chapter, analyze your instructional tools for their ability to engage the senses. Use a scale such as the one in Figure 2A that asks how well each tool prompts sensory input. Rate each instructional tool on a scale of 1 to 10. Be specific in your answers, giving the names of programs, models, materials, textbooks, and so on that your school is using.

(Note that the structure of the chart that follows, with its division into two columns, parallels the Two-Step Learning process. Although it's not essential to study the brain research behind Two-Step Learning now, it's recommended because it will help your committee(s) make better decisions. See page 3.2 and Appendices A and B. To see an example of this chart applied to a school, see page 2.5.)

On a second copy of the chart, plot the tools your school is considering. Abandon the idea of purchasing those that fall below the budget-cutting line. Save this money to meet budget-cutting goals.

Sensory Input Analysis Chart

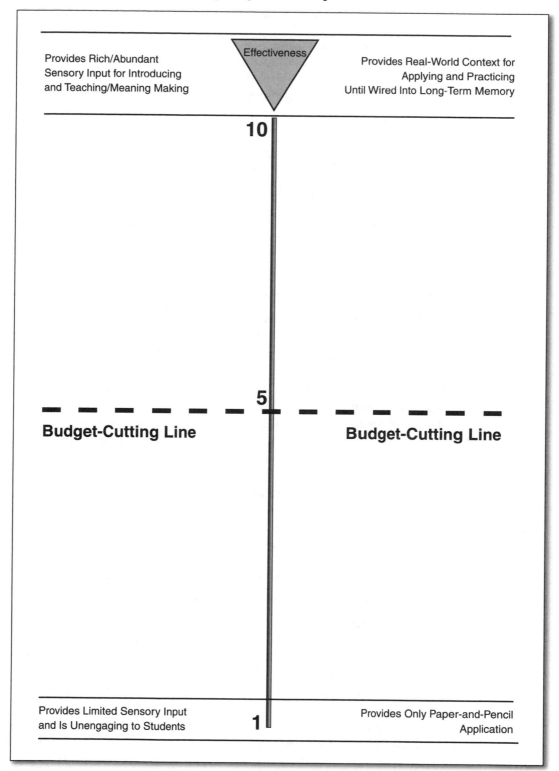

Figure 2A

Action Item C: Study your analysis

Ask the following questions about the analysis made in Action Item B:

a. Have we been as *honest* with ourselves as possible? Did we ask *what proof* we have in terms of student outcomes—objective and subjective? Did we provide a straightforward answer—no matter who likes what or who dislikes what?

b. Have we rated each tool based upon its *potential to stimulate physiological change in the brain* or upon what we believe we're *required to do* or *have always done*?

Make a list of tools that should be retired from use. List them in order of sensory input, least to more effective. Identify those that should be eliminated and, if necessary, what will replace them next year and each year thereafter.

Action Item D: Analyze past expenditures

Analyze past expenditures for each of the tools identified on the Sensory Input Analysis chart. Include one-time and ongoing expenditures and all related costs. For example, for worksheets, include not only the cost of the copy machine but also the paper and staff time. Also, calculate the ongoing cost for replacing consumables and lost or destroyed items for key programs. Be sure to include expenses dictated by current policies, such as the next round of textbook adoptions and the materials and training that accompany them. Ask your district budget person to help you dig out the information you need and to aggregate it in the clumps most valuable to you.

Create two new columns, one along the left side of the Sensory Input Analysis chart on page 2.3 and one along the right side. Record totals of last year's costs. See the examples in Figure 2B that follows.

Action Item E: Calculate the cost of continuing to purchase and replace all items under the "Budget-Cutting Line"

Be sure that your estimates are as accurate as possible and that you have included related costs.

Congratulations! You have just captured a sizable pool of money with which to meet your budget-cutting and program improvement needs. Such below-the-line expenditures can easily amount to $3,000 to $6,000 per classroom.

(Note for future reference: The Sensory Input Analysis chart is broken into two columns that match the discussion of the new, brain-based definition of learning introduced on page 3.2. Reading about the Two-Step

Example Sensory Input Analysis

| Provides Rich/Abundant Sensory Input for Introducing and Teaching/Meaning Making | | Provides Real-World Context for Applying and Practicing Until Wired Into Long-Term Memory | |

$ per Classroom	Examples:	Examples:	$ per Classroom
10			
$0	Study trips to *being there* locations	Study trips to *being there* locations	$0
$50	Immersion environments	Immersion environments	$25
$75	Hands-on of the real thing	Hands-on — building with real materials	$100
$25	Visiting experts with hands-on of the real thing	Social/Political Action and service projects	$0
$50	Simulations, individual, and collaborative	Simulations carried out in cooperative learning groups	$75
$100	Hands-on of representational items	Hands-on of representational items — building models	$250
$1250	Internet access and interactive CDs	Internet access and interactive CDs	$50

5

- - - **Budget-Cutting Line** - - - - - - **Budget-Cutting Line** - - -

$2500	Textbooks	? ? ?	$0
	Questions at the back of each chapter in the textbooks		
$3500	Worksheets	? ? ?	$0

| Provides Limited Sensory Input and Is <u>Un</u>engaging to Students | | Provides Only Paper-and-Pencil Application | |

1

Figure 2B

Learning process before you complete your decisions about instructional tools is highly recommended.)

Action Item F: Understand the politics of change

Understand the nature of the enemies of change. You'll meet them at every level.

At the school level, meet school culture—the way we do things here. A most formidable foe, culture has the deflection power of Teflon and the resiliency of DNA. Selecting brain research as a template for making decisions for budget cutting is a new idea. Don't underestimate the work to get it accepted and understood. Your challenge is to create a new culture with a new story line about our public schools, what Sally Goerner calls a "root metaphor."[3] This story line knits our world view together and shapes every thought, belief, and action—consciously or unconsciously.

Public education in America has never succeeded in replacing the factory model adopted from Prussia by Thomas Mann in Massachusetts as he and others struggled to create a free, universal, and compulsory educational system in the 1800s. Although we have railed against this system—solidified in the 1890s and unchanged since[4]—we have failed to come up with a replacement. (For more about the politics of change, see Notes on the Politics of Change at the back of this chapter, pages 2.16–2.17.)

Create a root metaphor for educating students at your school. It may be a single word or a phrase. Or you might develop a metaphor or catchy phrase for the program area addressed by each chapter. An example of a catch phrase for tools might be, "Different strokes for different folks," or "Different ways to run the race = Every child crosses the finish line." For curriculum work, it might be, "Learning is a two-step dance. Don't stop until the music ends."

Action Item G: Identify and challenge the sacred cows

Ask each teacher and involved stakeholder to list the sacred cows at your school—the things always considered untouchable. Identify the 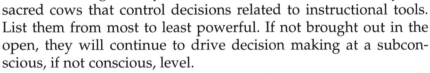 sacred cows that control decisions related to instructional tools. List them from most to least powerful. If not brought out in the open, they will continue to drive decision making at a subconscious, if not conscious, level.

Compare each sacred cow to what brain research demands for sensory input (see the Brain Research section starting on page 2.8). On every sacred cow (and related instructional tool) you list that is not compatible with brain research, write *CANCEL* across it in bold, red letters.

Next, compare the remaining sacred cows with the reality of today's students and their needs *now*, not in previous years. On any that no longer serve student needs now, write *CANCEL* in bold, orange letters. Circle in green any remaining item that you decide should move forward, not because it's a sacred cow but because it's the best approach to improving student outcomes in a time of decreasing funding.

Post the list in the staff lounge to encourage ongoing discussion. Sacred cows are not easily left behind. It will take time and plenty of reflection and discussion.

Action Item H: Use a zero-based budgeting approach

Zero-based budgeting requires that you start without any assumptions. Starting from scratch, one designs the program needed this year and then allocates the resources needed to implement this specific program. This is in contrast to starting with previous allocation patterns, and staff and tools, and adding on for the new things planned. The advantage of zero-based budgeting is that it forces you to start with what you want, not with what you have.

Start your zero-based budget list for instructional tools now. Add only those items that are compatible with the demand for rich sensory input. Expand the list as you study through each chapter of this book, prioritizing as you go.

Action Item I: Read brain research on the power of rich sensory input

After reading about the importance of rich sensory input in the pages that follow, consider what kinds of tools should be invested in. Reallocate some of the money cut from below-the-line items to buy the highest sensory items, particularly *being there* experiences. Set the amount of money to be reinvested in tools for next year.

Action Item J: Finalize your decisions

Finalize your decisions about budget cuts and necessary reinvestments. As you prepare to negotiate with the district office, include the following:

- A brief description of how these reallocations will improve learning for students and the brain research that supports such reinvestment
- A list of the variances from policy and law that you will need and how you will ensure achievement levels for students

If you get a *no*, don't be discouraged. Ask what it would take to turn the *no* into a *yes*. What actions or assurances must be included? Stay objective by keeping brain research in mind, especially the critical need for rich, multisensory input.

**Action Item K: Reallocate some money to
purchase sensory-rich tools**

Determine which subject areas are currently most adversely impacted by low-sensory-evoking tools. List these subjects in priority of need. Establish a long-term plan for eliminating and, when appropriate, replacing low-sensory tools, subject by subject.

Begin to research what tools are needed for the first priority area. Consider only those tools that elicit nine or more senses[5] and that have the highest cost-efficiency ratio. Place a small team in charge of ensuring this task is completed. (See ideas for high sensory input tools and the definitions of *being there* experiences and immersion environments in the Glossary.)

"We have at least 19 senses, not five."

Establish criteria for identifying what to purchase. For example, items that will do the following:

- Help teach and provide practice in applying a specific concept or skill identified in the curriculum (not just a fun hands-on activity)
- Engage at least nine senses
- Allow teachers to base their instruction in *being there* locations
- Provide the most cost-efficient tools for this particular concept or skill

If possible, delay purchasing new, sensory-rich tools until you have analyzed your curriculum (Chapters 8 and 9) and made the desired improvements. Be aware that this curriculum work will greatly affect your decisions about instructional tools.

**Action Item L: Before purchasing new tools,
plan and budget for inservice**

Plan and budget for sufficient professional development to ensure that the new tools are used effectively.

If you do not have sufficient money to provide the inservice necessary for every staff member to immediately reach proficiency with the new tool, do *not* purchase that tool until such resources become available.

BRAIN RESEARCH

The area of brain research that is critical for analyzing your instructional tools is enrichment theory—the importance of rich sensory input. We'll begin with a tale in two stories and end with a brain research summary.

A Tale in Two Stories[6]

These two stories, not unlike those each reader of this book has experienced, illustrate the 19 senses in operation.

Story 1

Our first story that illustrates the 19 senses is a simple one. Note that the event happened half a century ago but is still as vivid in the author's memory as it was the day it occurred.

Age eight, with her older brother, engaged in the thoroughly hopeless but intriguing task of attempting to dam up the creek south of the family home; sunshine on their backs, reflections dancing on the water; bare feet scrunching in the pebbly gravel and gooey mud; the tepid, slow-moving water with darting minnows disturbed by rearranging of rocks and the shovels full of smelly mud; the sweat from their efforts dripping down their faces; their laughter rippling across the creek; her brother's nearness; his patience with a little sister who "never stayed home like the other girls did"; the lessons of that day, the wonder of the creek, the beauty of family relationships.

Such moments of acute sensory awareness stay with us always.[7] For examples of information each of the 19 senses processed during such an experience, see Figure 2C on pages 2.10–2.11.

Story 2

Think back to an attempt to learn something "from scratch." For me, it was my first experience trying to "learn" computers. This is my story:

A colleague and his wife offered computer literacy classes in their home (at the time, they had more computers in their spare bedroom for such a class than the local university did). I was thrilled at the opportunity, paid my $30, and sat in the front row. My instructor-friend dove right into "what goes on inside the box." "Wow," I thought, "If I understood how things work, writing programs, never mind word processing, would be a piece of cake. This is the class for me!"

The story that unfolded boggled my mind. Whoever thought up this stuff in the first place?! If I didn't understand something, I raised my hand and kept it there until I got an explanation I could understand. The night was fascinating. I left the class thrilled to my toes. It was, after all, quite understandable conceptually despite its sci-fi veneer.

The next morning, my mother, who was visiting me at the time and whom I had tried to talk into coming with me to the class, asked reasonably enough, "Well, what did you learn last night?"

"Holy moley, Mom! You should have come. You would've loved it. It was our kind of workshop. He explained what goes on inside the box. It was fabulous!"

"Oh," she said, "So, just what does go on in there?"

"Well, when you plug it in and turn it on, it . . . ah, er. Now, let's see here, you plug it . . . turn it on and then. . . ."

Egad, how was this possible? I couldn't remember a thing except for my clear recollection that I understood it at the time. But nothing else stuck in my brain! I was horrified. I wanted and needed that information. What a waste! What happened?

The 19 Senses and the Input They Process

Sense	Kind of Input
Sight	Visible light
Hearing	Vibrations in the air
Touch	Tactile contact
Taste	Chemical molecular
Smell	Olfactory molecular
Balance	Kinesthetic geotropic
Vestibular	Repetitious movement
Temperature	Molecular motion
Pain	Nociception
Eidetic imagery	Neuroelectrical image retention
Magnetic	Ferromagnetic orientation
Infrared	Long electromagnetic waves
Ultraviolet	Short electromagnetic waves
Ionic	Airborne ionic charge
Vomeronasal	Pheromonic sensing
Proximal	Physical closeness
Electrical	Surface charge
Barometric	Atmospheric pressure
Geogravimetric	Sensing mass differences

Examples of Sensory Input From Story 1 (p. 2.9)

Reflections dancing on the water; darting minnows, dams breaking, and so on

Laughter, gravel scrunching; mud sucking; rocks clashing, splashing

Bare feet scrunching in the pebbly gravel; tepid, slow-moving water

Sweat dripping down faces; occasional splash of creek water

Smelly mud

Keeping balance wading in the deep gravel; moving rocks/mud

Rearranging rocks and shoveling smelly mud

Warm summer day

Pain . . . thankfully, none!

The vividness of the details; reflections dancing on water

The location of the creek—south of the family home

The warmth and power of the sun's rays

The refreshing feeling from being around water

Primal sense of smell—body odors, sweat, rotting vegetation

The nearness of the brother

The humidity of the creek eliminated any perceivable static electricity

The steady, unchanging atmospheric pressure of a calm summer day

Density (weight to mass) of material—pebbly gravel versus gooey mud

Figure 2C

Two things conspired against my getting the information into long-term memory. First, I had no prior experience with what goes on inside the black box, no mental post office box address for the information. Second, the only sensory input for this new learning was auditory and thus provided no context to help learn about the goings-on in the box. Consequently, the information evaporated from my short-term memory during the night.

Moral of the Two Stories

These simple stories underscore the fact that, over the millennia, the brain has evolved to process sensory input from the natural world—and it does so very powerfully, especially when the learner is in the process of doing, of acting upon the world, not merely observing it. *The bottom line is this:* Learning is the result of real physiological growth in the brain—growth stimulated by massive amounts of sensory input that heightens the brain's ability to seek patterns and develop programs.

An enriched environment is a learning environment that focuses sensory input—through all 19 senses—on the concept or skill to be learned. Maximizing sensory input is a fundamental goal when developing curriculum and planning instructional strategies for a number of reasons. *First,* input through the senses is the brain's only way to bring in information from the outside world; there are no shortcuts. *Second,* large amounts of sensory input enable students to grasp the concepts and information accurately and completely, thereby eliminating misunderstandings. *Third,* large amounts of sensory input are what causes physiological changes in the brain, resulting in the phenomenon called learning.

The instructional tools we use must provide input to as many of the 19 senses as possible. Traditionally, however, the instructional tools *most used* in the classroom—textbooks, workbooks, worksheets, and lecture—*provide the least sensory input.* Conversely, the two kinds of input *least used* in classrooms—*being there* and immersion—*provide the most sensory input.* (See Figure 2D.)

There Are No Shortcuts

Remember, *there is no such thing as bypassing the sensory system;* it is the bodybrain partnership's[8] way of taking in information. We cannot expect to set aside millions of years of evolution in favor of our traditional textbooks, lectures, worksheets, and, yes, computers. Simply put, worksheets don't make dendrites!

We must accept that words convey only limited meaning when our students lack relevant prior experience. Whether in speech or in print, understanding words demands bringing information to the situation.[9] Even in social conversation, a comment or question off the subject usually produces a "Huh?" response until the new topic is settled on and the relevant prior experience can be brought into focus.

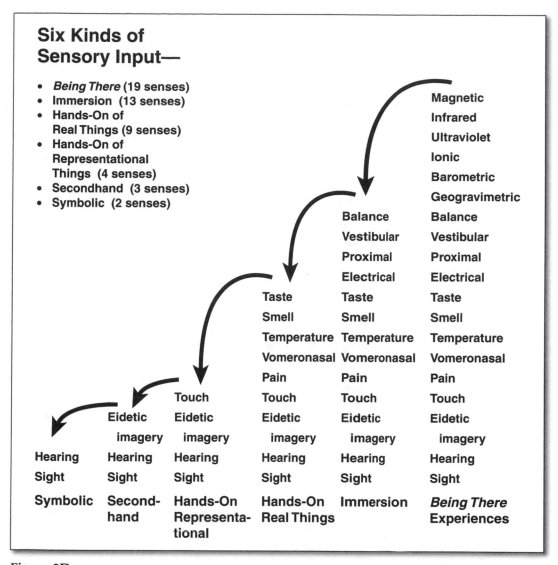

Six Kinds of Sensory Input—

- *Being There* (19 senses)
- Immersion (13 senses)
- Hands-On of Real Things (9 senses)
- Hands-On of Representational Things (4 senses)
- Secondhand (3 senses)
- Symbolic (2 senses)

					Magnetic
					Infrared
					Ultraviolet
					Ionic
					Barometric
					Geogravimetric
				Balance	Balance
				Vestibular	Vestibular
				Proximal	Proximal
				Electrical	Electrical
			Taste	Taste	Taste
			Smell	Smell	Smell
			Temperature	Temperature	Temperature
			Vomeronasal	Vomeronasal	Vomeronasal
			Pain	Pain	Pain
		Touch	Touch	Touch	Touch
	Eidetic imagery	Eidetic imagery	Eidetic imagery	Eidetic imagery	Eidetic imagery
Hearing	Hearing	Hearing	Hearing	Hearing	Hearing
Sight	Sight	Sight	Sight	Sight	Sight
Symbolic	**Second-hand**	**Hands-On Representational**	**Hands-On Real Things**	**Immersion**	***Being There* Experiences**

Figure 2D

John Medina, in *Brain Rules: 12 Principles for Surviving and Thriving at Work, Home, and School,* provides a powerful but simple summary of why rich sensory input is so critical:

All sensory encoding processes have these common characteristics:

1. The more elaborately we encode information at the moment of learning, the stronger the memory.

2. A memory trace appears to be stored in the same parts of the brain that perceived and processed the initial input.

3. Retrieval may best be improved by replicating the conditions sur-
rounding the initial encoding.[10]

Turning Lesson Planning on Its Head

As the author's two stories illustrate, the more massive the sensory
input, the better. Also, sensory input at real-world locations where the concept or skill is in use is a necessity, not a luxury. Brain research is very clear
on this issue and provides us with a new model of learning (Figure 2E).

Models of Learning—New Versus Traditional

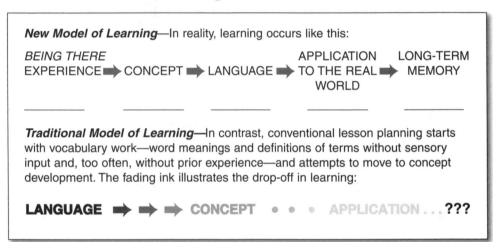

Figure 2E

Lesson planning that begins with *being there* experiences and rich sensory input through the 19 senses is a must. Evoking *maximum activation of
the brain is critical because it does the following:*[11]

- Overcomes inequities between advantaged students and those with
  more limited backgrounds (a *being there* experience gives all learners
  all the sensory input they need to seek and understand patterns and
  use what they are learning)
- Reminds students of previous related experiences so they can
  use that prior knowledge to help understand the current learning
  situation
- Illustrates the value of learning the concepts and skills and future
  possibilities for their using them, which is intrinsically motivating
- Provides the massive amounts of sensory input needed to rewire the
  brain in order to extinguish misunderstandings and wire up the correct information

- Enhances second language acquisition by heightening motivation, improving the accuracy of the understanding

By contrast, in the traditional model of learning, which starts with language and expects meaning and relevance to follow, sensory input is typically limited to hearing and sight in a classroom environment. This is light-years away from the real world where that knowledge or skill is used and valued.

Your goal to improve program while budget cutting is to flip these percentages—90% of the sensory input should come from *being there* and immersion experiences. Investing in *being there* experiences is a must. Refuse to invest in instructional tools that invite fewer than nine senses.

Secondhand input—principally reading, Internet, and video—becomes a *useful way to extend what has already been learned* through *being there* experiences supplemented with immersion, and hands-on experiences with the real thing.[12]

Brain Research Details

According to Marian Diamond, pioneer in enrichment theory, a number of changes occur when the brain is immersed in an enriched environment, changes that do *not* occur in indoor environments, such as classrooms, that shut out sensory input for all but a few senses, typically sight and hearing.

Changes in the brain associated with an enriched environment include the following:[13]

- Dendritic spines[14] grow, change shape, or shrink as we experience the world. Neurons grow larger. The brain becomes denser and heavier.
- As much as 20% more change occurs in brains in enriched environments compared to brains in sterile, boring environments.
- In sterile environments, the brain actually shrinks. "Use it or lose it" is a brain truism.
- A brain structures itself based on what it's asked to do and not do.[15] In other words, how we spend our time—what we do and don't do on a daily basis—shapes the brain's physical structure. Much of the inequity among learners comes from an expectation of the school that all students bring the same wiring, including the same prerequisite wiring[16] to learn what is taught. We then ask students to perform tasks for which they have no or insufficient wiring; this is cruel. We must teach students in ways that build that wiring. For example, if we want students to become creative problem solvers, we must give them not worksheets and homework assignments but real-life problems to solve that invite them to apply learning to real-life situations about the home and community.[17]

RESOURCES

This resources section provides two tools:

- Notes on the politics of change
- Sources for further study

Notes on the Politics of Change

As Walt Kelly observed, "We have met the enemy . . . and it is us." It lies in our unexamined beliefs and assumptions.

Shift in the Locus of Power. Understand that you're asking for a shift in decision making—from personal/social power to principle based. This often feels like a loss of power to those who have shaped policy, including spending decisions, in the past. Expect this sense of loss to fuel considerable political angst.

Also, be aware that local lore is filled with claims of "But this is required; we must do this." Once upon a time, I worked as a field services consultant for a state department of education. I was continually amazed at what school staffs believed was required by the state. Whether it was pure misinformation with the shelf life of uranium or something made up by a local Machiavelli to make people go his or her way, I could never determine. Even when I'd say, "But I am the state, and I'm telling you there is no such requirement," they were unswayed. Not until they saw it in print. So . . . make friends with your state's education code and related rules and regulations and the federal equivalents. Do your homework.

Expectation of Uniformity. At the district level, you'll meet the expectation of uniformity, a formidable foe. As your school begins to request exemptions to district policy in order to cut your budget, your requests will likely be seen as a challenge to the district's policies and leadership. Usually referred to as the "fairness" doctrine, in reality it is bureaucracy's demand for "sameness" or conformance. It is very powerful in school districts, as it is in the classroom. If Teresa is allowed to do or not do something, then why not the same for Ben? A rumor about inconsistencies in enforcement is considered dangerous. It undermines authority, brings down administrators and military officers, and is deeply feared. Or so it's often believed. Yet effective leaders have always found a way to make decisions appropriate to the moment and based on outcomes rather than conformance to a prescribed process or equal amount of dollars.

Likewise, schools with differing student needs should make different decisions when it comes to budget cutting (or any other decision). And let me repeat, this is a time of economic crisis. The "fairness" doctrine, which in reality gets implemented as the "sameness" doctrine, must be morphed into the "equity" doctrine and acceptance of the fact that sameness of input does *not* produce sameness of output or the same results in student achievement. Quite the opposite is the case.

Be patient with your district but hold firm to the equity doctrine because this is a time for new policies that will allow the stakeholders at your school the kind of latitude they need to make the best decisions.

When Good Intentions Go Awry. At the state level, education departments must temper the demands of politicians, at federal and state levels, who fall for solutions that sound good but whose implementation contains harmful elements. For example, No Child Left Behind created some horrific side effects. Forcing schools to focus so heavily on testing caused damage that will take years to fix, such as teaching to the test, increasing time for the three Rs, which resulted in reduction or elimination of physical education (PE) (and an explosion in obesity and poor fitness), and severe budget cuts in science, social studies, music, and the arts. According to brain research, these are catastrophic mistakes. Just ask students. They'll tell you the same thing.

As implemented, No Child Left Behind pushed education further away from implementing what brain research is telling us about how the human brain learns.

For Further Study

For further study about the importance of rich sensory input, see the following:

- *Exceeding Expectations: A User's Guide to Implementing Brain Research in the Classroom*, 4th ed. (2009), especially Chapter 1 and the importance of *being there* experiences.
- *Brain Rules: 12 Principles for Surviving and Thriving at Work, Home, and School* (2008) by John Medina. See Rule 9: Sensory Integration; especially note pp. 113–118.
- *Magic Trees of the Mind: How to Nurture Your Child's Intelligence, Creativity, and Healthy Emotions From Birth Through Adolescence* (1999) by Marian Diamond and Janet Hopson. Although published a decade ago, it has lost none of its clarity and relevance; it is an especially good resource for parents.
- *Human Brain and Human Learning*, 3rd ed., by Leslie A. Hart (2002), especially Chapter 8.
- *The Coming Great Change in Education* by Sally Goerner, Ph.D. (2009).
- *Closing the Achievement Gap: Using the Environment as an Integrating Context for Learning*, Executive Summary (1998) by Gerald A. Lieberman and Linda L. Hoody.

ENDNOTES

1. For more information on the 19 senses, see *Exceeding Expectations: A User's Guide to Implementing Brain Research in the Classroom,* 4th ed., Chapter 1, 1.6–1.16.

2. This thumbnail summary is accepted fact in the world of brain research. Early pioneers in enrichment theory include brain researcher Marian Diamond (see *Magic Trees of the Mind: How to Nurture Your Child's Intelligence, Creativity, and Healthy Emotions From Birth Through Adolescence*) and Leslie A. Hart, insightful translator of brain research to classrooms and schools (see *Human Brain and Human Learning,* 3rd ed., 2002).

3. See *The Coming Great Change in Education: A Practical Guide to How Scientific and Social Movements Are Remaking Our World and Our Schools* by Sally Goerner, Ph.D. (Black Diamond, WA: Books for Educators, 2006). This book has nothing to do with budget cutting but everything to do with the big picture of what kind of educational, and societal, reform is needed. A "must read" for administrators and teacher leaders not only when cutting budgets but also when layering in stimulus money, special grants, and post-recession expansion funds. The book will add a sense of urgency to your work.

4. One of my favorite educational historians is Michael B. Katz. See his book *Class, Bureaucracy, & Schools: The Illusion of Educational Change in America* (New York: Praeger Publishers, 1971). As Stephan Thernstrom points out in the book's foreword, "We hardly need yet another book to tell us that something is drastically wrong with the American educational system. But we badly need new insight into *how* that system came to be what it is. Without that, without a clear understanding of the historical roots of the contemporary educational crisis, real change is impossible."

5. The exception is nonfiction books that are sadly lacking in most schools. Gather desired titles through the school, city, and county libraries. Make friends with your librarians and give them a wish list well before you will need the books. Also, search for titles from free, downloadable sources such as www.bartleby.com.

6. I first shared these two stories and their application to brain research in *Kid's Eye View of Science: A Teacher's Handbook for Implementing an Integrated, Thematic Approach to Teaching Science, K–6* (1991). They are used here with written permission of the publisher.

7. The power of rich sensory input is simple to verify. Recall one of your most vivid memories from childhood. Analyze the scene in your mind's eye. You will discover input from most, if not all, of the 19 senses.

8. This is a key idea from brain research. It suggests that if we sat down to deliberately design an environment that would most thwart learning, we would design the traditional classroom, a relic from the 1840s.

9. As is often said, 80% of reading comprehension relies on prior knowledge. This is true in all areas of life, not just reading.

10. See John Medina's book, *Brain Rules: 12 Principles for Surviving and Thriving at Work, Home, and School,* 111–113.

11. Leslie A. Hart was the first to point out how critical rich sensory input is to the learning process—both pattern seeking and program building. See Chapter 8.

12. One cannot overemphasize the importance of full sensory input through *being there* experiences. See the definitions of *being there* and immersion-learning environments in the Glossary.

13. Diamond and Hopson, *Magic Trees of the Mind*, 26.

14. For an introduction to the physiological changes that create learning, see *Exceeding Expectations: A User's Handbook to Implementing Brain Research in the Classroom*, 4th ed. (2009), Chapter 1.

15. This message was first delivered to educators by Jane Healy almost 20 years ago. See *Your Child's Growing Mind: Brain Development and Learning From Birth to Adolescence* (first published in the 1980s). The message has changed little with time.

16. The greatest disparity in prerequisite wiring occurs in reading. For information about how to create wiring for decoding and comprehension, see Lindamood-Bell Learning Processes at www.lindamoodbell.com.

The Web site www.bartleby.com is an Internet publisher of literature, references, and verse providing students, researchers, and the intellectually curious with unlimited access to books and information on the Web, *free* of charge. Students can access and download thousands of free texts.

17. The real world is a strong motivator. We must find ways to reach beyond the contrived, artificial environment of the classroom.

ACTION SUMMARY CHECKLIST

_____ Action Item A: Establish the membership for this group.

_____ Action Item B: Analyze your instructional tools.

_____ Action Item C: Study your analysis.

_____ Action Item D: Analyze past expenditures.

_____ Action Item E: Calculate the cost.

_____ Action Item F: Understand the politics of change.

_____ Action Item G: Identify and challenge the sacred cows.

_____ Action Item H: Use a zero-based budgeting approach.

_____ Action Item I: Read brain research on the power of rich sensory input.

_____ Action Item J: Finalize your decisions.

_____ Action Item K: Reallocate some money to purchase sensory-rich tools.

_____ Action Item L: Before purchasing new tools, plan and budget for the necessary inservice.

3

Instruction—Organization and Use of Time

Time is both a blessing and a curse. We all have the same number of minutes in the day, but most of us complain we don't have enough. The only way to buy time is to organize it and use it more effectively and more efficiently.

OPTIMIZING ORGANIZATION AND USE OF TIME

Optimum organization and use of time for instruction has nothing to do with the clock, or bureaucratic convenience, and everything to do with the brain.[1] "Ah-ha's" cannot be scheduled on demand like setting one's alarm clock to ring at 6 a.m.

$ Cutting Potential — 3

Cost-Efficiency Ratio — 8

Instruction time must be organized and used in ways that enhance students' ability to complete their journey through learning as currently defined by brain research. This Two-Step Learning process is summarized in Figure 3A on the next page. For a fuller discussion, see the Brain Research section, page 3.7, and Appendices A and B.

Bottom line: Learning that enters short-term memory but does not become wired into long-term memory is dumped from short-term memory within minutes or hours. So, when learning is interrupted by inflexible schedules or classroom disruptions before learning is wired into long-term memory, the time spent is wasted.

Learning Is a Two-Step Process

LEARNING IS A TWO-STEP PROCESS[2]

Step One—Input stage: Pattern seeking and making meaning

First, the brain must detect/identify a pattern.

Second, the brain must make meaning of the pattern, including its relationship to other patterns.

and

Step Two—Output stage: Building programs to use what we understand

Begins with conscious effort (often with guidance) and then

With practice, becomes almost automatic and wired into long-term memory.

Figure 3A

Within each of these learning steps, the brain functions differently (see Figure 3B), needing varying amounts of time (and different instructional tools and curriculum) to move through each phase.

New Definition of Learning and Brain Activity

New Definition of Learning	Brain Activity[3]
Step One: Pattern Seeking	
• Identifying patterns.	Primarily right frontal lobes shifting to
• Making meaning, understanding.	Primarily left frontal lobes
Step Two: Program Building	
• Able to use learning with support.	Shift from front toward back of brain
• Ability to use the learning becomes automatic and wired into long-term memory.	Shift to back and lower and older brain structures

Figure 3B

ACTION ITEMS

Action Item A: Establish the membership

Establish the membership of the work group responsible for addressing organization and use of time. Set your meeting calendar. Survey your members to determine what information they might need to fully participate in this process. Be especially aware of the information needs of parents, community stakeholders, and classified staff members.

Action Item B: Analyze how instruction time is currently organized and used

Analyze how instruction time is currently organized and used *within your classrooms.* Involve all teachers. Percentages represent the percentage of the total day that each activity occurs. Note that time frames overlap: for example, classroom interruptions can occur during rigid time schedules.

Analysis of Organization and Use of Instructional Time

Organization and Use of Instructional Time	Percentage
• Rigid time schedules resulting in insufficient time for the task and failure to complete the Two-Step Learning process	_____
• Classroom interruptions, such as intercom announcements, students coming and going from various special programs	_____
• Classroom assignments, primarily of paper-and-pencil activities, that don't target where individual students are in the Two-Step Learning process, especially Step Two	_____
• Lack of integration so students study only one topic at a time (which fragments topics and limits time for science and social studies)	_____
• Spiral curriculum which results in fragmentation of content into meaningless pieces and much repetition (see Chapters 8 and 9)	_____
• Student inattention due to pent-up energy (see Chapter 6)	_____
• Low-sensory-input instructional tools that necessitate reteaching and remediation (discussed in Chapter 2)	_____
• Homework assignments that aren't targeted to where individual students are in the Two-Step Learning process	_____
• Grading homework[4]	_____
• Other time bandits _____	_____

Figure 3C

Make your best *guesstimate* of the percentage of the class or day that each of the above occurs. Multiply the percentage figure of an item times staffing costs for that area. The potential for "saving" money here is enormous. Although the dollars aren't real in terms of budget cutting, changes in organization and use of time in these areas can nonetheless buy a lot of improvement in student outcomes. (See the following for an example of this analysis.)

Example Analysis for Action Item B—How Instruction
Time Is Organized and Used Within the Classroom

This analysis shows how instruction time is currently organized and used *within classrooms.* Percentages represent the percentage of the total day that each activity occurs. Note that time frames overlap. For example, classroom interruptions can occur during rigid time schedules.

Example Analysis of Organization and Use of Instructional Time

- Rigid time schedules resulting in insufficient time for the task and failure to complete the Two-Step Learning process   80%
- Classroom interruptions, such as intercom announcements, students coming and going from various special programs   10%
- Classroom assignments, primarily of paper-and-pencil activities, that don't target where individual students are in the Two-Step Learning process, especially Step Two   90%
- Lack of integration so students study only one topic at a time (which fragments topics and limits time for science and social studies)   95%
- Spiral curriculum which results in fragmentation of content into meaningless pieces or repetition or both (see Chapters 8 and 9)   25%
- Student inattention due to pent-up energy (see Chapter 6)   40%
- Low-sensory-input instructional tools that necessitate reteaching and remediation (discussed in Chapter 2)   95%
- Homework assignments that are not targeted to where individual students are in the Two-Step Learning process   90%
- Grading homework[4]   10%
- Other time bandits _____   _____

Figure 3D

Action Item C: Prioritize the list

Prioritize the list generated in Action Item B. Then, assign each item a timeline specifying when you will begin to improve it. Work for a unanimous agreement.

Action Item D: Analyze how well instruction time fits the learning needs of students

How well do these time frames support teachers in ensuring students complete Two-Step Learning? Determine what changes will make their time with students more effective and efficient.

In elementary schools, examine the daily schedules teachers are asked to maintain. These can be as rigid as time in secondary departmentalized class periods. What flexibility are teachers permitted on an ongoing basis?

Also, how is time currently organized and used by your *specialists* within the time schedules they have been given. How effective is the specialists' time with their students in terms of ensuring students complete Two-Step Learning?

And, just as important, how does the coming and going of students to specialists' programs affect students (those in specialist programs and those not) in terms of the classroom teachers' attempts to complete Two-Step Learning in the classroom?

As you examine your school's practices, consider this scenario: All specialists are scheduled into the same grade level at the same time; art, music, physical education (PE), technology, and library specialists all work with, for example, only fourth graders during the same time period. The fourth-grade teachers and the specialists—as a team—then work out the number of minutes needed and how the students are grouped. Such week-by-week planning based on content to be learned replaces the standard weekly mini-slices of time; however, the time per month per grade level would stay the same. This could also allow for special days or weeks when grouping could be based on talent levels (aspiring artists, gifted musicians, etc.), or for double the minutes every other day to allow for completion of projects or more in-depth explorations. For examples of scheduling of specialist time, see the Resources section at the back of this chapter, pages 3.8–3.11.

The beauty of such a schedule is that it provides weekly (at least) grade-level team-planning time, plus it makes specialists' time more effective and efficient. It also eliminates the interruption to classroom work created by groups of students coming and going.

Revisit this issue each year until the work of each specialist is optimized for their students and also enhances students' classroom work rather than disrupting it.

In departmentalized schools, examine the extent to which the x-minutes-a-period structure allows for Two-Step Learning. What degree of flexibility is routinely given teachers to ensure learning through Step Two?

There is no gentle way to say this—the 45-minute period day is the antithesis of adequate time for learning and the traditional practice least compatible with what we now know about how the human brain learns.

As you examine your school's practices, consider the learning outcomes achieved by intensive block, 4 × 4 block, A/B plan, modified block, one subject at a time for seven weeks, and other hybrid models (see page 3.10).

Revisit this issue each year until failure to reach Step Two in learning, and wiring it into long-term memory, is the exception rather than the typical outcome.

Action Item E: Separate the sacred cows and folklore from actual law

Programs such as Chapter 1, English as a Second Language (ESL), and special ed have been in existence a long time, certainly long enough to create sacred cows and folklore about what's required and what's not.

Identify and list the sacred cows and folklore relevant to this committee's work. Assign a member of your group to bring an up-to-date version of law and regulations for each of the federal and state programs that receive significant amounts of money at your school. Have him or her highlight sections relevant to the issues of organization and use of time and staffing. If a sacred cow has no basis in law, determine how to get rid of it and move on.

Summarize your discussions on a two-column chart: Sacred cows and folklore in one column and how to eliminate or replace them in the second column. Post this in the room when you meet.

Commit yourselves to controlling the controllables. Although you may not be able to control federal and state mandates, you can control how you organize and use your time to do those tasks.

Action Item F: Identify any necessary changes in school policy or tradition

In addition to others you might eliminate, revise, or add, consider adding a policy that describes the degree of latitude a classroom teacher and teacher-specialist teams may exercise on a day-to-day basis to optimize student progress through Two-Step Learning.

For examples of ways to improve the organization and use of time analyzed for Action Item B, see the Resources section at the back of this chapter, pages 3.8 through 3.11.

Action Item G: Involve your district office and school board

Start early; involve the district office staff person who will be responsible for approving your policy change requests in staff and community meetings. In your written request for a change in policy, be specific—what you intend to do and why, what related law and/or regs stipulate, how your school will evaluate the impact, and so on.

Action Item H: Create an action plan

Create an action plan to address organization of time both within the classroom and by specialists. You might begin with a subject area the entire school will address or one for a grade level or set of grade levels or for a school within the school. Be specific—what, who, timeline, and how progress will be monitored and evaluated. Be sure you have specifically addressed organization and use of time for both classroom teachers and teacher-specialist teams as an integrated whole.

Action Item I: Commit to increasing your strengths

Organization and use of time is *always* more effective and efficient when people are working within their strengths. Commit yourselves to a comprehensive, ongoing professional development program that expands the range and depth of each staff person's strengths. This is your first line of defense against eroding student outcomes during budget cuts. See Chapters 4 and 5.

Be sure you provide sufficient professional development to ensure that staff are fully prepared to make the most of the changes in organizing and using time (as developed for Action Item H).

Develop a long-term plan. Set a percentage of your budget for such professional development and maintain it year by year. Rule of thumb: 5% of your staffing budget (including benefits) per year. Note: If staff turnover at your school is high, the need for staff development will be ongoing.

BRAIN RESEARCH

Learning as a two-step process is not new, either to brain research or to practice in the classroom. Leslie A. Hart was the first to describe it in 1983 in the first edition of his landmark book, *Human Brain and Human Learning.* Russian-trained neurologist and American immigrant Elkhonon Goldberg describes the shifts in activity in the brain as a learner moves from first encounter to practiced use in *The Executive Brain: Frontal Lobes and the Civilized Mind* (2001).[5] And no serious discussion of brain research since has failed to mention the pattern-seeking[6] operation of the brain nor that we develop mental (usually mental-physical) programs[7] for using what we learn as we wire learning into long-term memory.

> *Optimum organization and use of time for instruction have nothing to do with the clock and everything to do with the brain.*

Implementation of Two-Step Learning was first documented in the classroom in 1985. A fascinating DVD, *I Can Divide and Conquer,*[8] shows how a fourth-grade teacher took 50 students from the beginning of Step One of learning through proficiency and wiring into long-term memory of Step Two—A to Z all in one day—single digit and double digit divisors, fractional remainder, story problems, and so on. Yes, one full day, with her 30 fourth graders, plus 20 more fifth and sixth graders who had failed to master long division. It's a brilliant illustration of the power of organizing and using time, our most expensive and rare commodity, so that it supports Two-Step Learning.

The assessment results of the first Division Day are worth noting. In pre- and post-testing (the day before and the day after), students went from near zero to proficiency—every student through single-digit divisors and most through double-digit divisors. When tested again at the end of the year, their scores remained the same or improved. When the students were in their senior year in high school, they gathered for a party to reminisce about that day. They all remembered it with startling clarity and felt it was one of the best school days they ever had.

Throughout the 1980s and 1990s, Division Day was replicated in districts across the country. The result was always the same . . . completion of Two-Step Learning and wiring into long-term memory. Imagine the time saved . . . not only in fourth grade but in fifth, sixth, seventh, eighth, and remediation on through high school and even college. Imagine, just one day and the job is done—once and for all!

The same idea was applied to multiplication in a week, also replicated across the country, and to addition[9] in two days (see *Mission Addition*, a DVD). And don't forget the possibilities for punctuation in a half day (use of commas and periods or colons and semicolons, or capitalization).

For a description of the two steps of learning, see Appendices A and B. A word of advice: Study this material carefully because it has huge implications for curriculum (Chapters 8 and 9) and testing (Chapter 10).

Sources for Further Study:

- Appendices A and B.
- *Human Brain and Human Learning,* 3rd ed. (2002) by Leslie A. Hart, especially Chapters 4 and 7 through 10.
- *Exceeding Expectations: A User's Guide to Implementing Brain Research in the Classroom,* 4th ed., vol. 1, especially Chapters 4 and 5.
- *The Executive Brain: Frontal Lobes and the Civilized Mind* by Elkhonon Goldberg, especially the discussion of the gradiental and distributive view of the brain, page 70.

RESOURCES

The two resources included are as follows:

- Ways to improve organization and use of time for Two-Step Learning
- Myths about organization and use of time

Ways to Improve Organization and Use of Time for Two-Step Learning

In Elementary Schools

- Make rigid time schedules more flexible:
  - When necessary to ensure completion of Two-Step Learning or eliminate wasting time, take recess at any time during a window of 20 minutes before or 20 minutes after the regularly scheduled recess.
  - Trade lunch time with a class from another grade level in order to stick with a project until completion or go to lunch early when

the time remaining isn't sufficient to begin another block of learning.

    ○ Morph daily requirements for minutes per subject into weekly totals in order to allow for such decisions as teaching science in the morning during math time because a particular area of science is ideal, *or* teaching social studies in the morning as part of the language arts block when a historical novel has gripped the interest of students, *or* doubling up on social studies one week (with no science) and then vice versa, and so forth.

    ○ Schedule two brief exercise periods in the classroom rather than taking one regular recess period. (Such flexibility could be stated in school policy. Parameters could be added, such as being contingent on the nature of the exercises and their adequacy to release pent-up energy and reset students' emotional state for learning and limiting their frequency to once or twice a week.)

• Reduce classroom interruptions:

    ○ Restrict intercom messages to a 10-minute period after school starts, five minutes after lunch, and five minutes before the final bell.

    ○ Create a message box just inside the door of each classroom where messages can be delivered silently without interrupting the teacher.

    ○ Establish a hand signal to be used at the door for "I need to talk to you right away," which conveys the message but allows the teacher time to get to a point in the lesson where the impact of an interruption would be minimized.

• Reduce classroom interruptions by specialist programs:

    ○ Schedule all specialists to work with the same grade level at the same a time so all students in a classroom work with specialists during the same time period.

    ○ To create longer periods of time for team planning or budget cutting, create a rotating schedule as follows:

12:00–12:45	Classroom A—music Classroom B—PE Classroom C—art Classroom D—technology	1:30–2:15	Classroom A—art Classroom B—technology Classroom C—music Classroom D—PE
12:45–1:30	Classroom A—PE Classroom B—art Classroom C—technology Classroom D—music	2:15–3:00	Classroom A—technology Classroom B—music Classroom C—PE Classroom D—art

In Departmentalized Middle and High Schools

The most urgent change needed in departmentalized settings is changing time schedules and the underlying cultural belief that the job to be done is teaching subjects. The job to be done is ensuring that learning about the world occurs—through both steps of the Two-Step Learning process to wiring into long-term memory.

Here are some models to explore, most of which have been around for decades and have considerable track records:[10]

- One course at a time—students study one subject all day for seven weeks. The Swedish university system has used this model for more than 100 years, and a military academy in Fort Union, Virginia, has done so for more than 30 years. This model is popular with students and faculty. Yet critics complain that it makes it difficult for transfer students. However, I think that most local taxpayers would argue that their money should be spent to the best advantage of local students. Mobility by some shouldn't overrule what would best work for the many.
- Intensive block—students study two subjects for 60 days. This model is also popular with teachers and students and worried over by critics because of students who transfer in or out.
- Modified block is a catchall name for many different plans: for example, four courses in four days with a traditional five- to seven-period day on Fridays for electives or a single period running every day throughout the year for such electives as foreign language, music, and other courses that would benefit from brief daily sessions.
- A/B Plan—often referred to as the Alternating Day Schedule because students attend six or eight classes over a two-day period, that is, three or four courses a day. While this model roughly doubles the time per class period, it is still inflexible, and an hour and a half is still often insufficient to complete Step Two of learning.
- Hybrids—a mix and match of various models

Two other challenges affecting organization and use of time in departmentalized settings are institutional flexibility and creating a sense of community.

The challenge when providing flexibility is resisting the siren call for consistency. However, when we become more confident and resolute in basing our decision making in brain research rather than in tradition and bureaucratic convenience, we will be able to organize and use time more effectively for student learning.[11]

The sense of community, so vital in a learning environment, requires smaller units of people trying to relate to each other. School-within-a-school settings allow community-building time to be spent effectively.

Myths About Organization and Use of Time

There are many timeworn practices in organization and use of time that have no basis in brain research. None. Zilch. Here is but a beginning list:

- Rigid time schedules (e.g., reading from 8:30–10:00, recess 10:00–10:15 in elementary schools and 45-minute periods in departmentalized settings)
- Allocation of a set number of minutes per day per subject
- Homework in every subject every night for elementary grades (This practice adds to the instructional day and thus to learning; in truth, homework in elementary schools is a burden to parents and interferes with student play and exercise time. In middle and senior high, it detracts from exploration of the world of work and experiencing how societal and governmental systems work.)
- Spiral curriculum, which adds up after years of pieces and repetition
- Sameness in organization and use of time to ensure sameness of outcome

ENDNOTES

1. That no two brains are alike is an undisputed fact in the field of brain research. Not in structure, not in chemistry, not in wiring due to prior experiences. Also undisputed is that the time needed to learn something varies for each brain and varies greatly. Thus, providing the same amount of time to all and expecting the same outcome is bureaucratic insanity, yet another example of sameness not leading to equity.

2. Learning as a Two-Step process was first conceptualized by Leslie A. Hart, who was the first to coin the term "brain-compatible" learning. See *Human Brain and Human Learning*, 3rd ed. (2002), especially Chapters 4 and 7 through 9. Also, see *Exceeding Expectations: A User's Guide to Implementing Brain Research in the Classroom*, 4th ed. (2009) by Susan J. Kovalik and Karen D. Olsen, especially Chapters 1 and 2.

3. Elkhonon Goldberg was one of the first brain researchers to provide the physical evidence of the shifts in brain activity as the brain moves through the learning process. See *The Executive Brain: Frontal Lobes and the Civilized Mind* (2001), 70. Also, see *Spark: The Revolutionary New Science of Exercise and the Brain* by John J. Ratey, M.D., with Eric Hagerman (New York: Little, Brown and Company, 2008), 42.

The amount of physiological growth in the brain needed to wire the shifts illustrated in the graphic will not occur from listening to a lecture, reading a chapter in a textbook, answering questions at the back of the chapter, and completing a ditto for homework.

4. The vast majority of homework assignments are an absurd waste of time—for both students and teachers. See "Rethinking Homework," *Principal*, January–February 2007 and *The Homework Myth: Why Our Kids Get Too Much of a Bad Thing*, both by Alfie Kohn.

5. Goldberg, *Executive Brain*, 70.

6. The descriptor of the brain as a pattern seeker is another well-established fact in the field of brain research. From the 1980s to the first decade of the 21st century,

the concept is more strongly reinforced. See *Human Brain and Human Learning,* 3rd ed. (2002) by pioneer Leslie A. Hart, especially Chapters 4 and 7 through 10, and more recently, *On Intelligence: How a New Understanding of the Brain Will Lead to the Creation of Truly Intelligent Machines* by Jeff Hawkins with Sandra Blakeslee (2004); *Brain Rules: 12 Principles for Surviving and Thriving at Work, Home, and School* by John Medina (2008), 115; and *Spark: The Revolutionary New Science of Exercise and the Brain* by John J. Ratey, M.D. (2008), 41–42.

7. Leslie A. Hart was the first to describe the end point of learning as the acquisition of useful programs. See *How the Brain Works: A New Understanding of Human Learning, Emotion, and Thinking* (New York: Basic Books, 1975).

8. This 55-minute DVD is a captivating account of optimal organization and use of time—one teacher with 50 students, 30 being introduced to long division for the first time and 20 who had failed to learn it as fourth graders, in one extended day. Every middle and high school in America should be using the principles of effective organization and use of time illustrated in this DVD. No more need for semester-long remedial math courses. A companion implementation book comes with the DVD, both available through Books for Educators, www.book4educ.com.

9. *Mission Addition* is a DVD illustrating the same principles of effective organization and use of time as illustrated in *I Can Divide and Conquer* but this time with 85 second graders learning addition. Also available through Books for Educators, www.book4educ.com

10. There are dozens of Web sites that discuss various models for changing time schedules in departmentalized situations. The debate has raged for more than half a century. For an overview, see www.phschool.com/professional_development/block_scheduling/introduction.html.

11. Institutional flexibility in departmentalized settings is long overdue. To begin your exploration, see www.ascd.org/publications/newsletters/infobrief/summer07/num50/New_Options_for_the_Modern_Student.aspx.

ACTION SUMMARY CHECKLIST

_____   Action Item A: Establish the membership for this group.

_____   Action Item B: Analyze how instruction time is currently organized and used within your classrooms.

_____   Action Item C: Prioritize the list and create a timeline.

_____   Action Item D: Analyze how well instruction time fits the learning needs of students.

_____   Action Item E: Separate the sacred cows and folklore from actual law.

_____   Action Item F: Identify any needed changes in school policy or tradition that may be needed.

_____   Action Item G: Involve district office and school board.

_____   Action Item H: Create an action plan.

_____   Action Item I: Commit to increasing your strengths.

4

Staffing

People are the biggest cost in any service enterprise. Thus, the effectiveness and cost efficiency of staff is vital. In education, the most cost-efficient version of staffing is creating highly skilled classroom teachers who do the following:

$ Cutting Potential—8

Cost-Efficiency Ratio—6

- Teach effectively the first time, thus avoiding the need for remediation.
- Bring a variety of skills and knowledge to the table so that they can partner with subject area specialists. (This is important because it allows specialists to differentiate their time in order to best use the breadth and depth of their expertise for students—and for staff.)

No staffing plan is complete without a discussion of professional development. No matter who the staff are or what their written job descriptions may be, the outcomes of

Remediation is always more expensive than doing the job right the first time.

their labor—student growth and achievement—can be significantly enhanced by a vigorous and rigorous, ongoing professional development program. For a discussion of designing a professional development plan, see Chapter 5.

ACTION ITEMS

As you examine staffing at your school, think of yourself as a sculptor working clay—the best results come from taking some resources from here and adding some there. Some of what you cut will help you meet your budget requirements, and some should be reinvested so that the end result is an improved program and better outcomes for students.

Action Item A: Establish the membership

> "The trick is in what is emphasized. We either make ourselves miserable, or we make ourselves strong. The amount of work is the same."
>
> —Carlos Casteneda

Establish the membership of the committee responsible for working on staffing. Set your meeting calendar. Survey your members to determine what information each might need to fully participate in this process. Be especially aware of the information needs of parents, community stakeholders, and classified staff members of the work group. Be sure to make the information available as needed.

Action Item B: Set your course

Begin by establishing some basic principles to guide your work. Include a rationale for each. For an example, see the discussion of staffing principles on pages 4.7 through 4.8. Work toward unanimous agreement as you develop these principles. Post them on the wall during each meeting of this group.

Action Item C: Find out what is

List the current staff positions. Consider grouping positions in a way that makes analysis of their contribution to the program easy to see at a glance, such as in the categories in Figure 4A on page 4.3. Include the cost of benefits. Calculate the percentage of the entire staffing budget each category represents. Are these percentages in line with the educational needs of your students?

Ask district office staff to assist you.

Action Item D: Compile a list of positions that will become vacant

Compile a list of positions that will become vacant during the remainder of this year. Compute the total savings for salary and benefits by category. Record the amounts resulting from this task in the column on the right (see Figures 4A and 4B).

Assign a group member to compile estimates for next year; update weekly.

Staffing Analysis—What Is
(Schools With Self-Contained Classrooms)

Certificated Staff	Current Costs	Anticipated Openings
Regular classroom teachers		
Subject area specialists, for example, art, music, PE, technology		
Remediation staff, for example, reading, math, ESL		
Special education staff		
Support staff, for example, librarian, counselor, nurse		
Administrative		
Other _____		
SUBTOTAL		
Classified Staff		
Regular classroom aides		
Remediation program aides		
Special education program aides		
Support positions directly related to the classroom instructional program, for example, copying materials, parent outreach		
Other support positions with students, for example, playground, hall, and lunchroom supervisors		
Administrative support, for example, office personnel		
Transportation (including bus stop and traffic guards)		
Maintenance and repairs		
Other _____		
SUBTOTAL		
TOTAL		

Figure 4A

Staffing Analysis—What Is (Departmentalized Schools)

Certificated Staff	Current Costs	Anticipated Openings
Teachers of classes required for graduation		
Teachers of college-bound and advanced placement classes		
Teachers of vocational ed classes		
Teachers of other electives		
Remediation staff, for example, reading, math, ESL		
Special education staff		
Support staff, for example, librarian, counselor, nurse		
Other support positions with students, for example, lunchroom supervisors and security staff		
Administrative staff		
Staffing for competitive sports		
Other _____		
SUBTOTAL		
Classified Staff		
Regular classroom aides		
Remediation program aides		
Special education program aides		
Support positions directly related to the classroom instructional program, for example, copying materials, parent outreach		
Administrative support, for example, office personnel		
Transportation (drivers, mechanics, traffic guards, etc.)		
Maintenance and repairs		
Other _____		
SUBTOTAL		
TOTAL		

Figure 4B

Action Item E: When a vacancy occurs, don't let the chips lay as they fall

In other words, don't let the vacancies determine which service(s) won't be continued. How a reduction in staff occurs should be a deliberate decision, not determined by the departing footsteps of a particular staff member. Your work group should decide how and where that reduction in staffing will occur and recommend how that workload should be redirected.

> "We would accomplish many more things if we did not think of them as impossible."
>
> —Vince Lombardi

See "Thoughts on Dealing With Vacancies" in the Resource section at the back of this chapter, page 4.8.

Create a specific plan for each vacancy; provide more than one option if feasible. Remember to cut more money than necessary to meet budget-cutting goals so that there will be some funds to reinvest in areas that will significantly increase student outcomes.

Action Item F: Reinvigorate your volunteer program

Volunteers are the lifeblood of every successful community. Schools are no exception. More than the actual work they perform, it is their commitment to the mission of the organization that is so valuable, inspiring students, other volunteers, and paid staff as well.

Consider questions such as the following:

- Is our volunteer recruitment program as vigorous as it could be? If not, what steps can we take to improve and grow in this area?
- Is the program well coordinated so that staff can depend on their volunteers?
- Is the training we provide adequate to enable volunteers to make valuable contributions to our program?
- Are the tasks assigned to volunteers meaningful and important to the mission of the school? If not, why not? How can we improve in this area?
- Does our volunteer training and support program make volunteering a satisfying and self-fulfilling experience that motivates participants to continue volunteering?
- Does the training carry over into the lives of volunteers outside of school, proving of value to them at home in their role as parents, at work, and/or in the community? If not, how can we improve the quality and relevance of our training?
- Are we using our volunteer corps to create a hiring pool of skilled classroom aides, thereby shortening the time it takes to provide our teachers with expert help? Are we hiring substitute teachers from this pool?

> *"The volunteer world is a laboratory for self-realization."*
>
> —Unknown

Establish criteria for selecting a volunteer to coordinate the volunteer program. Consider such qualities as high energy, recognized and respected leadership skills, a sense of moral authority, dependability (their word is their bond), commitment to helping staff create and maintain excellence, good verbal and written communication skills, tactful but able to say what needs to be said, liked and respected by fellow volunteers and staff, and so on. If the task is large, consider selecting two coordinators who can work well together with a feasible split in the tasks to be done.

Be sure to create the needed support for the coordinator(s) you select, for example, a work space with telephone and computer, one hour a week of office secretarial support (this is more for access to needed information and technology than for actual typing or copying time, which could be done by other volunteers), a room for volunteers to gather when they arrive early or have a project to complete, and so forth.

This position, well staffed and supported, is the most cost-effective staffing decision you can make. Assign a member of your group to make sure that the coordinator has the support he or she needs.

Ask a parent artist to make a poster of the above quote; hang it in the coordinator's work space and wherever volunteers gather.

BRAIN RESEARCH

It doesn't take a brain scientist to point out that remediation is *always* more expensive than doing the job right the first time. But we should read some of the sociological research on the damaging impact on students that occurs when they are singled out for remediation. However well intended, being in remedial classes makes students feel inferior. Elizabeth Cohen[1] recounts a study of first-grade students. Each could rank their classmates by reading ability and insert themselves into that ranking. With minor exceptions, each student's list matched the teacher's. Cohen points out that if students at the bottom don't lose their remedial or Chapter 1 label before third grade, they will carry the belief that they're "dumb" throughout their schooling and lives, expecting low success levels and low-paying jobs. And self-esteem programs do not change this perception.[2]

Staffing for remediation competes directly with resources for effective first teaching. At some point, it becomes a downward spiral—more remediation is needed because first teaching becomes less and less effective.

RESOURCES

Resources provided here include thoughts on the following:

- Setting basic principles for staffing
- Dealing with vacancies
- More fully using subject area specialists' expertise

Thoughts on Setting Basic Principles for Staffing

Establishing, and sticking with, a set of basic principles under which the committee will work is critical to your success. For Action Item B, consider the following:

Principle 1: Effective first teaching. Effective first teaching means doing the job right the first time—ensuring students achieve competence and wiring that competence into long-term memory. Make it your number one priority. I have yet to see[3] a classroom of students, from inner city to rural, that cannot be effectively taught by one well-trained and well-equipped classroom teacher (the exception, of course, is special education, especially for the emotionally and severely handicapped). However, over the past 50 years, the system has bypassed classroom teachers and has instead invested in remediation rather than in making each classroom teacher more effective. Partly, this is due to funding requirements of programs such as Chapter 1, which require funding be spent only on targeted students and on the early categorization and isolation by special education programs.

It is past time to rethink this funding strategy.

Principle 2: Effective use of specialists' time and expertise. Although it can be argued that not everyone is born with sufficient talent in music or art to adequately teach these subjects in the classroom, it can also be argued that it is not unreasonable to expect that a college-educated adult should know at least as much in every subject as what we expect K–6 students to learn and be able to do. If we expect students to stretch themselves, so should teachers. Also, with training, one can teach others to excel beyond one's own talents.[4] Again, however, over the past 50 years, the system, as a matter of policy, has opted to invest in staff around the classroom teacher.

You may think that I'm preparing grounds to argue that subject specialists should be eliminated. I am not. But I do suggest that using specialists the same way for all classrooms for all students is a criminal waste of resources, talent, and expertise, not to mention money. Classroom teachers should, with training and support, partner with specialists to do the best job they can *before* specialist expertise is factored in. This would not only increase the time students have for such subjects (with both classroom teacher and specialist providing instruction) but also allow the specialist to differentiate instruction, especially for those highly talented in the subject. For example, see the discussion on pages 4.9–4.10.

Principle 3: Invest in the future. Effective first teaching and effective use of specialists' time and expertise won't happen overnight. It will require better decisions about organization and use of time plus a strong commitment to professional development and plenty of it . . . and on an ongoing basis.

If you don't now have an intensive professional development program for new teachers and ongoing training for continuing teachers, prepare to reallocate monies here. At a minimum, plan to spend 5% of your staff budget (salaries plus benefits) each year.

The more successful your classroom teachers, and the greater their satisfaction with teaching, the less turnover there will be.[5] A core of strong classroom teachers will anchor many improvement efforts.

Principle 4: Invest in high return professional development. Shepherd your money carefully. Expect every dollar to make an observable and tangible difference in the classroom.

Thoughts on Dealing With Vacancies (Action Item E)

As mentioned earlier, the intent is not to toss people out of their jobs but rather to capture job positions after they have been vacated.

For Classroom Teacher Positions: Don't wait for the bureaucratic system to find candidates. Be proactive. At least half of any staff knows of a college student majoring in education. Contact those students well in advance of their graduation date. Ask them to visit your school and, if they like what they see—especially the support for them as new teachers[6]—provide them the necessary paperwork to apply. Follow up with them. Ensure that your school has a large pool of qualified candidates from which to select and provide them with an intensive inservice training and support program through their first two years.

> "If we do what we've always done, we'll get what we always got."
>
> —Anthony Robbins

For Classroom Paraprofessional Positions: Canvass your staff. Invite any teacher whose students (such as 90% of those attending at least eight months) consistently gain one grade level each year to consider the option of working without a classroom aide. If the teacher agrees, shift his or her aide to the newly vacated position. As a thank-you for that teacher's contribution to budget cutting, split the salary savings, on a one-time basis or for two years, with that classroom teacher. For example, 25% to the teacher to be used for his or her training, *being there* experiences, immersion resources, and Two-Step Learning materials as he or she requests (and is approved by the principal). Use the remaining 75% to reach your budget-cutting goals and/or for the school's professional development plan. For the next three years, if student achievement in that teacher's room is the same or better, continue to allocate 10% to that classroom teacher. (In my opinion, this is the best approach to "merit pay." Allocations to directly support excellence is the right message to give, and because most teachers use their own money to buy what their school can't provide, it is, in effect, a merit pay increase to a teacher's salary.)

For Maintenance Staff Positions: Consider leaving positions open.[7] Invite teachers and their students to take on those responsibilities. If enough classrooms say yes, save half of the salary and benefits for budget cutting and divide the other half equally among the classrooms taking on the work to be used for class study trips to *being there* experiences that are the basis of large chunks of study. For each trip, give students two locations to choose from, either of which the teacher considers a powerful context from which to teach the selected content. (Note: This can also open up lessons on going green and alternatives to toxic cleaning chemicals. Do your homework; know what union issues apply to your school.)

Thoughts on More Fully Using Subject Area Specialists' Expertise (Action Items D and E)

Consider questions such as the following:

- Are we fully using the depth and breadth of our specialists' talents and skills? Or have we assigned them to equal time per classroom to provide primarily entry-level instruction to students classroom by classroom? (The higher the turnover rate of students, the more basic the instruction tends to remain.)
- If you answered no to the first question, are there areas of specialist content (and how to teach it) that most classroom teachers could incorporate into their classroom? Would doing so result in higher-level content training in some classrooms, thus enabling specialists to utilize more of the depth and breadth of their expertise? Would it result in better student outcomes in that content area? What would be the cost for the needed professional development and instructional tools? How long would it take?
- What specialist content would be the most difficult and least cost-effective for regular classroom teachers to attempt to incorporate into their classroom?
- Are we using our specialists to provide inservice for our staff—teachers and classroom aides? If not, why not? How can we begin to

extend the specialists' knowledge and skills throughout the school so that they have the time to provide higher level instruction to talented students?

- Are the basic skills being taught effectively the first time so the need for remediation is kept to an absolute minimum? If not, what inservice and instructional tools do classroom teachers need? Could specialists' time be organized more effectively, for example, to provide weekly inservice training for classroom teachers (one subject area at a time) or to focus only on the most needy (such as in reading) or on the most talented (such as in art and music)?

Answers to these questions will help you begin to prioritize where to start planning for staff professional development.

Here are some examples of differential use of specialist time:

Options for Art: Every staff has born artists who, with weekly 30-minute training by the art specialist, can become proficient enough by the end of one year to become their own "specialist"—at least at beginning levels of student instruction. This would open up real flexibility in specialists' time. If all teachers at a grade level, for example fourth grade, agreed to become their own art specialist for beginning level skills, the specialist could then serve fourth grade in a support role, mentoring, helping lesson plan, coaching, and so forth during the first semester. Specialist time with the other grades would increase.

During second semester, the specialist could cut back on time with the other grade levels in order to work with especially talented fourth-grade students, providing advanced instruction and/or work with individual fourth-grade classes on projects relating to current curriculum topics.

Options for Music: The entire staff joins the staff chorus for weekly 30-minute rehearsals and voice training. Music specialist time can then be allocated much like the art specialist as described above. By year two, classroom teachers are able to teach beginning level skills in their classroom. During the first semester, the music teacher works intensively with the most gifted and talent vocal students, producing a special Christmas show. During second semester, the music teacher works with grade-level choirs that work toward a spring concert.

These kinds of approaches allow a school to ratchet up the quality of the program, notch by notch, without spending a single penny. The budget committee's job is to acquire the necessary variances to account for time by the year, not by the day or week.

A side benefit is that this kind of approach gives staff the opportunity to model the joy of learning. It can also become the basis for a staff community service project, for example, Christmas caroling at a homeless shelter, art presents for a senior facility, and so on.

Thoughts on Staffing in Departmentalized Settings

Staffing in departmentalized situations, particularly in high schools, is subject to far greater push-pull forces between the inertia of bureaucracy and protectionism of unions than that found in self-contained environments. A book such as this can only observe that neither group puts the interests of students first. For example, bureaucracy tends to treat all staff as interchangeable parts to be handled the same, despite unique talents and interests; mostly the job is dealt with as a numbers juggling task. Unions tend to hold fast to rules such as last in–first out and do so without consideration for the unique talents and interests of staff, such as who can teach advanced math or science classes, for example, calculus or nuclear fusion. Seniority also tends to lead to a class system in which longtime staff get assigned plum positions (usually interpreted to mean college prep and advanced placement classes) while new, less experienced staff are assigned to remedial and other non-college-bound classes.

> "Every block of stone has a statue inside it, and it is the task of the sculptor to discover it."
>
> —Michelangelo

In such a milieu, budget cutting produces a difficult environment, especially if one also hopes to improve or even maintain program quality.

Perhaps this economic downturn will inspire both camps—those ensnared in bureaucratic inertia and those leading the district unions—to recast the thinking of their organizations and put students' needs and concerns foremost on their agendas. As the saying goes, when mom and dad fight, the kids lose. And under the current mind-sets, budget cutting will be wielded like a chain saw rather than a scalpel.

ENDNOTES

1. See *Designing Groupwork: Strategies for the Heterogeneous Classroom,* 2nd ed., by Elizabeth Cohen (New York: Teachers College Press, 1994). Although the book is more than 10 years old, it is a gold mine. Particularly noteworthy are the sections on why providing time for collaboration is so crucial and how to develop curriculum and assignments that are appropriate for collaborative work.

2. See Alfie Kohn, *Punished by Rewards: The Trouble With Gold Stars, Incentive Plans, A's, Praise, and Other Bribes* (New York: Houghton Mifflin, 1993) and *The Homework Myth: Why Our Kids Get Too Much of a Bad Thing* (New York: Da Capo Books, 2006).

3. During my years with the California State Department of Education, I was lead reviewer for hundreds of Program Quality Reviews, in elementary, middle, and high schools—in all, more than 6,000 classrooms throughout the state. From huge urban schools to tiny, one-room rural schools, effective first teaching stood out in sharp relief. The difference was not size, location, or student body; the difference was always a teacher who was well trained and well equipped with the

appropriate tools and instructional strategies. The 700+ teachers who passed through the Mid-California Science Improvement Program (MCSIP) taught me another valuable lesson: It isn't just the innately gifted teachers who can become effective first teachers, although they too certainly improved. Time and again, I watched teachers, considered by their schools to be average or even marginal, become outstanding. The necessary ingredients included the following:

- Commitment to improving student outcomes
- Willingness to improve—to learn, try, be coached, learn from mistakes, to try again . . . in a never-ending cycle in the pursuit of excellence
- A comprehensive professional development program to take them there

4. Examples are everywhere: The highly effective diving instructor whose own equilibrium system became completely disoriented whenever her head got lower than her knees. The high school music teacher who was not a performer herself but was an extraordinary voice trainer—her challenges in acquiring musical expertise actually made her a more expert teacher of voice. The principal in a Texas school who required every K–5 teacher to learn and teach an instrument of his or her choice—although the sounds coming from some of the rooms weren't pretty, students thrived on the opportunity and went on to far exceed their teachers' talents and abilities. (Most exciting was that academic achievement skyrocketed despite the fact that nothing changed except the advent of music instruction.)

5. High staff turnover takes a grim toll on improvement efforts, funding, and student outcomes. Not unlike the plot in the movie *Groundhog Day*, for a principal, it's like repeating one's first year over and over again: Every September, playing catch-up with new staff while dreaming a far-off dream of mounting an improvement effort.

6. Some years ago, the curriculum director of a school district in Southern California recounted this experience: Because the district was growing rapidly and hiring dozens of new teachers every year, it decided to invest heavily in supporting them—making them successful so they didn't quit teaching. It directed all of its Mentor Teacher Program resources, and more, to help new teachers. By the third year, their director of personnel arrived early at a work fair to find a huge line from his desk out the door. There were no other lines that morning. He was stunned, the more so because his district had a history of scratching and scraping to find teachers. When he asked why there was so much interest in his district this year, each candidate had the same answer: "I heard that your district has a good training program for first-year teachers."

Smart investments continue to pay dividends. The district's investment in new teachers attracted the best candidates ever to apply, and more of them not only stayed in the profession but also stayed with the district.

7. There is also much to be said about the value of students learning life skills, among which are maintaining a clean and organized personal space and household (in this case, a classroom).

I can still recall the training that home economics majors received at the university campus I attended. Each home ec major had to live in the home ec department's "house" on campus. Every household task was meticulously taught, coached, and supervised: monthly stripping and rewaxing floors (who does that anymore?!), weekly cleaning and reorganizing of the refrigerator, menu planning for the week (remember those leftovers?), nighttime dishes and sanitizing the kitchen in preparation for a new day, almost daily dusting and vacuuming, making your bed *before* you went to the bathroom to start the day, and so forth. There was an everyone-home-for-dinner-at-six curfew, and the schedule never varied—not for a homecoming game, not for midterms or finals.

In short, students were taught the patterns and programs of the job of cleanliness and organization, and they were taught through to the end of Step Two of the learning process. Although they meowed viciously, the students learned the business of running a household as if it were a business—the high standards of employment for a homemaker and home ec teacher alike.

Years later, the curriculum director in a heavily migrant, low income, non-English-speaking K–6 district and I included this life skill focus into a New American Schools Development Corporation (NASDC) proposal. We wanted the moon and proposed redirecting all special funding (all legally) to make the following happen:

- Lower class size to 20
- Extend the student year by 10 days
- Extend the staff year by 30 days with an 8% annual salary increase
- Rearrange the calendar into five study periods separated by 10 days and shortened summer and lengthened Christmas vacations
- During every break but Christmas, five days of vacation and five days of paid professional development time (training and preparation time) for teachers
- During every break but Christmas, access to 10 days of community schools programming (attendance optional) for students

Students were given responsibility for their own classrooms and their portion of the common areas of the school, which included handling repairs, painting over graffiti, daily cleaning, and so on. Students could hire a job out (and learn from the repair-man), enlist parent help (and pocket the money), and/or learn to do it themselves (with licensed supervision).

Funding for the eight percent increase in teachers' annual salaries for the extended year largely came from elimination of classroom aide positions funded by Chapter 1, ESL, and migrant funds.

Funding for the community schools program and monies for *being there* experiences came largely from students taking responsibility for maintenance and repairs.

ACTION SUMMARY CHECKLIST

_____   Action Item A: Establish the membership.

_____   Action Item B: Set your course.

_____   Action Item C: Find out what is.

_____   Action Item D: Compile a list of positions that will become vacant.

_____   Action Item E: When a vacancy occurs, don't let the chips lay as they fall.

_____   Action Item F: Reinvigorate your volunteer program.

5

Professional Development

$\mathbf{A}$s Robert Frost observed,

"Two roads diverged in a yellow wood,
And sorry I could not travel both. . . ."[1]

In Frost's case, the choice is an existential struggle and perhaps, just perhaps, there will be another opportunity later in life to choose again. In the case of education versus the taxpayer, it's an either/or policy decision. These two paths in education funding—which cannot be traveled simultaneously due to budget constraints—are

1. investment in classroom teachers to create effective first teaching

or

2. investing in resources *outside* of the classroom—remediation and subject specialists—to make up for what should but doesn't happen *in* the classroom.

Starting in the 1960s, public education in the United States chose this second road as part of the war against poverty. In hindsight, perhaps that wasn't the best public policy decision—useful in the short run but problem ridden in the long run. It's another case of

$ Cutting Potential—1

Cost-Efficiency Ratio—9

5.1

yesterday's solution becoming today's problem. Staffing for remediation competes directly with dollars for effective first teaching and undermines improvement efforts.

To compound the problem, the United States lags behind its western counterparts in investing in professional development for its teachers.[2]

This must change.

PROFESSIONAL DEVELOPMENT IS A SURVIVAL IMPERATIVE

Companies that are successful over time understand that investing in their people is a survival imperative, not a luxury. Those organizations that "learn how to learn" as a group[3] confront and conquer the challenges that arise in an ever changing landscape and emerge the stronger because of them. For the most part, educational bureaucracies are having great difficulty making this leap. Those that fail to do so will fail to meet the challenges of the 21st century and their students. The stakes couldn't be higher.

Professional Development That Works

Professional development that works carries every staff member through Two-Step Learning—to automatic, daily implementation of new skills and knowledge. Compare Approaches A and B (Figures 5A and 5B, respectively) and their results.

Professional Development Outcomes—Approach A

Learning as a Two-Step Process[4]				
	Step 1 Pattern Seeking		**Step 2** Program Building	
	Making meaning, understanding (input)		Using what is understood (output)	
Learning Processes	**Identify Patterns**	**Make Meaning**	**Apply With Assistance**	**Use Automatically**
Kind of Workshop	Learner Outcomes		Learner Outcomes	
One-shot workshops	Introduction, reminder of topics drop out of short-term memory		?	0
Multitopic workshops (e.g., before school)	Understanding to the level of ability to apply is unlikely		?	0
Schoolwide curriculum workshops	Little or no understanding of specifics for own grade level		?	0

Figure 5A

Professional Development Outcomes—Approach B

	Learning as a Two-Step Process			
	Step 1 Pattern Seeking		**Step 2** Program Building	
	Making meaning/ understanding (input)		Using what is understood (output)	
Learning Processes	**Identify Patterns**	**Make Meaning**	**Apply With Assistance**	**Use Automatically; Wired Into Long-Term Memory**
Kind of Workshop	Learner Outcomes		Learner Outcomes	
Short (2 hours), single-topic, grade-specific workshops taught through modeling, collaboration, multimedia, classroom visits, and coaching	Can identify patterns in topic; understands elements of implementation for grade level		Practices elements of topic in collaborative groups and gets feedback from peers	
Workshop content determined by levels of use[5]	Large amount of content "makes sense" and is usable by each participant		Develops a personal implementation plan	
Followed by grade-specific coaching	Anticipation of follow-up coaching forces clarity of what is to be implemented (for both presenter and participant)		Works on implementation elements with coach one-on-one and as a grade level Learning Club; implements elements daily and reaches automatic performance before a new workshop topic is scheduled	

Figure 5B

Approach A, a traditional, low-budget design, is cheaper than Format B—in the short run. However, when analyzed through the lens of Two-Step Learning, Approach A is extremely costly in the long run. If a professional development program doesn't support staff until they have mastered the new skills and can apply them with almost automatic ease on a daily basis, then the professional development program has failed and all resources expended—time, money, and goodwill—are wasted. And, in the process, the program has probably annoyed its participants.

ACTION ITEMS

Action Item A: Establish the membership of the committee responsible for working on staffing

Establish the membership of the committee responsible for working on professional development. Ability to maintain confidentiality is a critical selection criterion. Set your meeting calendar. Survey your members to determine what information each might need to fully participate in this process. Be especially aware of the information needs of parents, community stakeholders, and classified staff members of the work group. Be sure to make the information available as needed.

Action Item B: Analyze the effectiveness of your recent professional development program

Using the chart in Figure 5C, analyze the kinds of workshops and their outcomes conducted for your staff during the past year. After analyzing the information, identify your priorities for improving future professional development.

Professional Development Analysis Form

Learning as a Two-Step Process[4]				
	Step 1 Pattern Seeking		**Step 2** Program Building	
	Able to seek for understanding (input)		Able to use what is understood (output)	
Learning Processes	Identify Patterns	Make Meaning	Apply With Assistance	Use Automatically
Kind of Workshop	Learner Outcomes		Learner Outcomes	

Figure 5C

Action Item C: Commit to developing and providing ongoing, comprehensive professional development

Establish principles to guide you as you plan, implement, and evaluate your professional development program. As you do so, consider the following elements:

- Consistent annual allocations—5% per year (salary plus benefits by categories such as those in Figure 4A on page 4.3)
- Content aimed at improving each teacher's ability to provide Two-Step Learning for his or her students in all subject areas
- *Organization of content and instructional strategies aimed at ensuring that each teacher completes his or her Two-Step Learning process for the key concepts and skills of each training session*
- Dedication to the twin principles of effective first teaching and developing and making best use of individual staff members' talents and skills
- A healthy disregard for the "sameness" principle in favor of the principles of equity and excellence
- Based in strategies that create cascading improvements rather than strategies based solely on prioritization of greatest need
- Includes regular volunteers

Post your version of these elements in the room during every group meeting.

Set priorities; do not underestimate the time, effort, and cost to complete an area of training to the point that the behaviors are incorporated into classroom life. For a discussion of these elements, see Thoughts on Designing a Comprehensive Professional Development Program for Classroom Teachers on pages 5.10 through 5.12.

> *Remember . . . the changes we seek will not be easy. If they were, they would already have been made.*
>
> —Anonymous

Rule 1: Stick with an area until the job is done. This means that the content presented has moved through both steps of the Two-Step Learning process—*until the knowledge and skills are fully implemented in every classroom.*

Action Item D: Set high standards for each inservice session

Insist that every inservice session meets the following criteria:

- Utilizes the best trainers available
- Is taught using strategies to ensure Two-Step Learning
- Focuses simultaneously on both the content of the subject and how to teach it—curriculum content and instructional strategies
- Is grade-level specific in both curriculum content and instructional strategies

- Models effective instructional strategies, particularly those that lead to effective first teaching
- Is provided through frequent, small amounts of time rather than through infrequent, large chunks of time (such as all day)
- Includes an evaluation of the session based on how well Two-Step Learning was employed by the presenter and how well participants moved through Step One and at least halfway through Step Two; focuses on the effectiveness of the inservice in terms of changing teacher behaviors in the classroom rather than upon what content was "learned" (what can be performed in the classroom versus what is talked about)
- Provides follow-up coaching after each session to ensure each participant completes Step Two of Learning

> *If we expect our students to learn and be able to do something, then so should we expect each of our teachers to do so.*

Assign a member or team from your group to work with each inservice presenter to ensure that each of the above criteria is adequately met. Contact the presenter at least three weeks prior to the session to give him or her adequate time to make the necessary adjustments in content and presentation strategies.

Have the same member(s) follow the progress of follow-up coaching.

Refuse to use or reuse presenters who do not meet your criteria and expectations.

Action Item E: Change the ethic about professional development

Most staff look upon onsite training as a dreaded infringement on their time. Such resentment is too often justified by one-size-fits-all sessions that insult and bore some, seem "out there" and frivolous to others, or seem pointless and useless to those that can't find a unifying thread or any relationship to current direction set by the school or the district. Others fail to notice that the shoe fits, and some find the content unremarkable because the session was poorly presented.

Whatever the reasons, some legitimate and some not, a common perception is that implementation after a workshop is optional. This must change.

Creating a professional development program that meets the criteria of Action Items A and B is the first step in changing the ethic about staff development and the most important one. *As a school community, all of us must be held personally accountable for implementing what is learned—staff, parents, and community members.*

Second, discuss this issue as a staff.

Third, assign a member of your group to follow up with those who coach after each inservice session. Solicit their opinions about staff willingness to implement new behaviors in the classroom and what they think is needed to improve implementation. Randomly interview several teachers who do not implement key elements of the inservice and those that do. What are the lessons to be incorporated into planning of future inservice sessions?

Have the group member assigned to follow-up report on the effectiveness of coaching and the degree of implementation to the work group every two months. Take all steps necessary to improve each staff member's implementation of key inservice elements. This is key to the efficacy of your leadership, to effective use of reallocated monies, and to ensuring that student outcomes improve during a budget-cutting era. If necessary, postpone plans for a future inservice topic in order to have sufficient resources to ensure full implementation of current topics.

Action Item F: Strategize, don't just prioritize

Usually, prioritizing for professional development by greatest need is the best approach. But not always, particularly when funding is tight. When you select content for professional development, consider these three metaphors:[6]

- Key domino—The problem that if fixed would significantly affect or even eliminate numerous other problems
- Log jam—The log that must be removed first so that the entire pile of snagged trees (problems) can move down the river . . . the most significant barrier in this classroom and/or school
- Foundation—What needs to be in place to support the existence of the improvement strategy you want implemented

Analyze the possibilities. Remember, a quality professional development program has the biggest and longest-acting potential to improve outcomes for students.

See "Thoughts on Designing a Comprehensive Professional Development Program for Classroom Teachers" in the Resources section at the back of this chapter, page 5.10.

Create two lists of professional development possibilities: One based on greatest need and the other based on strategy using the above metaphors. After considering both lists, identify the areas of professional development you wish to address and rank them in the chronological order that will be most effective. If your budget is insufficient to handle a meaningful part of the task, wait until sufficient funding becomes available. Providing half a loaf is a waste of time, money, and patience.

Create a budget for the areas you can afford this year. Next year, revisit this list, make any needed changes, and budget for the next year. Repeat this cycle annually thereafter.

Ask a parent artist to make a poster for you that says the following:

Drop the pebble. Start the ripple.

Display it on the wall wherever your group meets to discuss staffing and plan professional development.

Action Item G: Acquire the best trainers available

Often this means hiring an outside consultant; sometimes it means having one of your specialists fill the bill. But whoever you choose, remember that the greatest expense in professional development is the time and goodwill of those being trained. Don't take second best when it comes to selecting a trainer.

Start a list of potential presenters by subject or program area. Assign a member of the group to update the list on a weekly basis. Track fees and travel expenses.

Action Item H: Create "free" time for professional development

Create time for grade-level inservice sessions that doesn't drain your budget by scheduling the specialists you have in blocks as discussed earlier on page 3.9. This frees up all the teachers at the same grade level for professional development, coaching, and to collaborate as a team. Such scheduling allows professional development time to occur during the workday and by grade level (thus allowing for grade-level specific content) and eliminates the need for substitutes. It also provides the opportunity for frequent, short sessions that are more productive than infrequent, long sessions.

Action Item I: Include coaching[7]

Make sure that every day of inservice training is followed by *three coaching sessions* for each participant. Plan for additional coaching for those needing more time and support to complete implementation.

Assign a group member to work with the coaches after the second round of coaching to get an estimate of how much more coaching time is needed. Pull needed funding from that allocated for future professional development topics.

Action Item J: Involve your curriculum director

Involve your curriculum director in scheduling professional development districtwide so that, after the initial trainings for each group (teachers or aides or janitors or ____), there will be continuing opportunities for incoming staff to receive trainings sufficient to bring them to the same level of proficiency as those hired earlier. Such centralizing of inservice needs makes catch-up training minimal for each school.

BRAIN RESEARCH

The most relevant brain research for designing a comprehensive professional development program is Two-Step Learning (see pages 3.2 and 5.10).

RESOURCES

To think about designing professional development from a fresh perspective, consider the following thoughts:

- More fully using subject area specialists' expertise
- Designing ongoing professional development for paraprofesionals
- Designing a comprehensive professional development program for teachers
- Status of professional development in the U.S.

Thoughts on More Fully Using Subject Area Specialists' Expertise

Consider questions such as the following:

- Are we using our specialists to provide inservice for our staff—teachers and classroom aides? If not, how can we begin to extend the specialists' knowledge and skills throughout the school?
- Are the basic skills being taught effectively the first time so the need for remediation is minimal? If not, what inservice and instructional tools do classroom teachers need? Could specialists' time be organized more effectively, for example, to provide weekly inservice training for classroom teachers (one subject area at a time) or to focus only on the most needy (such as in reading) or on the most talented (art and music)?

Answers to these questions will help you begin to prioritize where to start planning professional development.

For examples of differential use of specialist time, see pages 3.9–3.10 and 4.9–4.11.

Thoughts on Designing Ongoing Professional Development for Paraprofessionals

Consider questions such as the following:

- How well trained are the individuals in these positions?
- Are their content knowledge[8] and instructional skills sufficient for them to function as teachers of small groups or only as one-on-one

tutors? Reality check: By the end of five years, classroom aides (with lesson planning assistance from their teacher) should be as effective at small-group instruction as their classroom teachers.

- In our bilingual settings, are all staff good English models? If not, consider reassigning such staff members to other positions, such as community liaison. Or provide the training necessary to help them improve their English.

If you are not happy with your answers to any of the above questions, consider this a priority area for reallocating funds. Rule of thumb: Allocate 5% of the amount budgeted for paraprofessionals (including benefits) to an ongoing training program. Do so every year.

Thoughts on Designing a Comprehensive Professional Development Program for Classroom Teachers

Invest in who you can become. Allocate 5% of your total staff costs (salary plus benefits) to professional development.

The following observations about professional development come from my experiences with the Mid-California Science Improvement Program (MCSIP). A 10-year, $3 million effort funded by the David and Lucile Packard Foundation to improve science education based on brain research and the ITI (now called *HET*) model, the 700+ K–6 participants who stayed in the program through at least one three-year cycle taught us a great deal. Here are some of those lessons.

Insist That Every Session Models Two-Step Learning. No more "covering" information. Instead,

- Work with the presenter ahead of time and agree on what your teachers will be expected to *do* with the content and focus on those actions and skills.
- Provide tools for follow-up implementation.
- Provide some time during the inservice for teachers to begin their action plan while they have the trainer available to answer questions.

Model what Two-Step Learning looks like, sounds like, and feels like and what it does *not* look like or sound like or feel like.

Strike a Balance on the "Chicken or the Egg" Dilemma. Question: Which is more important for a teacher to have—subject area content knowledge or instructional skills? Answer: *Both are critical.* And they should be taught simultaneously. Poor instructional strategies will kill otherwise engaging content.

Well-taught nothing is still nothing. Recommendation: Provide *at least 5 to 10 days* a year of content training (with instructional strategies built in).

Emphasize Subject Content Training in Real-World Contexts. Select one content area at a time. Recommendation: As heretical as it sounds, don't start with one of the basic skills. Chances are that you have been thumping away at them every year, in which case, the wisdom of Anthony Robbins comes to mind: "If we do what we've always done, we'll get what we always got." Plan strategically, not where the need is greatest.

Based on the MCSIP program, I strongly recommend you start with science because it is the easiest medium for applying brain research, especially the importance of rich sensory input and the Two-Step Learning process. It also provides concepts that readily integrate all content areas that become high-interest projects for applying the basic skills. Engaging content makes students want to read[9] and eager to use math to find answers to questions that intrigue them.

It's also the easiest subject in which to model the power of *being there* experiences—for all ages, kindergarten to adult.

Be Grade-Level Specific. Content should be that which each teacher is expected to teach. Generic trainings frustrate, anger, and bore. They are a waste of money. It took us a year in MCSIP to learn that even two presentations— one for primary and one for intermediate—was a waste of time and money. It wasn't until we offered seven workshops—one for each grade level K–6—that teachers began to move. The contrasting metaphors are a carpet bomb versus a laser-beam targeted smart bomb.

You may think this is impractical and too costly. However, from my 10-year experience with the MCSIP[10] program, it is the most effective thing you can do for student outcomes and the most cost-efficient for program improvement.

Coaching After Every Session Is a Must. Coaching is the guided practice for Step Two of learning. If you can't "afford" to provide coaching, don't waste money on a workshop that can only provide Step One content. "Talking" about a topic does *not* equal being able to implement it. Were that so, our school programs across the country would look vastly different than they now do. Coaching helps move people from understanding to competently doing and implementing.

The more stressful the environment, the more difficult it is to make a change in one's behavior in the classroom. Coaching helps teachers turn the power of coping behaviors into new behaviors that make things work better and reduce tension.

Avoid Inservice Aimed at How to Use a Textbook Series or Program. Provide inservice that aims at expanding teachers' knowledge of the subject and how best to teach it—*not* just how to implement the newly purchased textbooks and materials.

This shift in staff development content will make the money you now spend on professional development significantly more cost-efficient because it increases understanding of the job, and the training content is cumulative. In contrast, inservice on how to use a newly adopted textbook series or simulation program is rendered obsolete the minute such programs are substantially revised or replaced. This is particularly important for the basic skills.

Before finalizing the engagement of any trainer, have a member of your committee review the content of the proposed training. Do not proceed with the training unless you are convinced that the content is focused on expanding teachers' knowledge of both subject content and instructional strategies.

Include All First- Through Sixth-Grade Teachers in Training for the Basic Skills. A common misconception is that the basic skills are the sole domain of first- and second-grade teachers, and thus, teachers at other grade levels are exempt from any responsibility to teach or reinforce basic skills at levels below the grade they teach. Wrong. It is everyone's responsibility in public education to ensure that our citizens are literate and fully capable of engaging in the significant debates of the day. It is the responsibility of everyone in education to ensure that our citizens can make informed judgments about both policy and funding issues, the environment, and who their leaders should be.

Basic skills training for grades 1 through 6 is important because the following is true:

- Every upper grade teacher has a student or two reading (or writing or doing math) at a primary grade level.
- Teacher assignments shift among grade levels over the years. When upper grade teachers get reassigned to primary grades, their students can't wait until they become effective first teachers of reading, writing, and math.

Have a member of your committee review the content of basic skills trainings. Make sure that the trainer will address how these skills can be taught at upper grades, for example, by making suggestions for materials, teaching through content areas, use of volunteer tutors (student and adult), and so forth.

Training in the basic skills is a perfect example of an inservice topic that could be coordinated across schools. Keep your district office curriculum director involved in your planning.

Status of Professional Development in the U.S.

American public schools have underfunded and under-planned professional development for decades. For a comparison of professional development funding and approaches in other countries, see "United States Is Substantially Behind Other Nations in Providing Teacher Professional Development That Improves Student Learning" by Robert Johnston and Chloe Louveouzo (Washington, DC: National Staff Development Council, February 4, 2009).

For a thorough discussion of how to design a comprehensive, ongoing professional development program, see *Coaching for the HET/ITI Model: Delivering on the Promise* by Karen D. Olsen, Chapters 4 through 7, pages 53–124.

ENDNOTES

1. Robert Frost, "The Road Not Taken," *The Poetry of Robert Frost* (New York: Holt, Rhinehart and Winston, 1916), 105.

2. R. C. Wei et al., "Professional Learning in the Learning Professions: A Status Report on Teacher Development in the United States and Abroad" (Stanford, CA: National Staff Development Council and the School Redesign Network, Stanford University, 2009). Also available at http://www.nsdc.org/about/news/ study2_4_09_release.pdf.

3. See "Becoming a Collaborative Learning Society," *The Coming Great Change in Education: A Practical Guide to How Scientific and Social Movements Are Remaking Our World and Our Schools* by Sally Goerner, Ph.D. (Black Diamond, WA: Books for Educators, 2006).

4. See page 3.2 and Appendices A and B.

5. Karen D. Olsen, *Coaching for the HET/ITI Model: Delivering on the Promise* (Black Diamond, WA: Books for Educators, 2009), Chapters 1 through 3.

6. Olsen, Chapter 5: "Working With Adults: Determining What Content to Present."

7. Olsen, 177–179.

8. I once worked in an elementary district that made continual enrollment toward a degree a prerequisite for continued employment as a classroom aide. In a district well known for challenges—students were low income, highly migrant, and largely non-English speaking—the requirement hit like a bombshell. Most of the aides had not completed eighth grade, and only a few had a high school diploma. The district provided two weeks of GED preparation (attendance voluntary and no stipend); all passed the exam. The community outreach coordinator held a session for all who wanted help with their college application and course planning. She also went with the group the first night of class to make sure everyone found their way. Only three aides quit; education as a career didn't interest them, and they readily found jobs in other fields. A year later, all agreed that their enrollment in classes was good modeling and gave the right message to

students. Some years later, almost a quarter of the group had completed a four-year degree and had become teachers.

9. When teaching remedial reading at high school and intermediate grades in the 1970s, I was struck by the truth of Daniel Fader's comment that many kids don't learn to read, not because they can't, but because they don't want to. From their perspective, there's nothing to be gained by it. The reward is having another boring worksheet to complete. See *The New Hooked on Books* (New York: Berkley Publishers, 1981).

10. Over the 10 years of the MCSIP program, we learned numerous hard but invaluable lessons about how to train generalists to become proficient science teachers. Most critical were the need for grade-level specific content in all of our trainings and modeling of effective instructional strategies built into the format, especially the importance of basing curriculum content and instructional strategies in *being there* locations.

ACTION SUMMARY CHECKLIST

_____ Action Item A: Establish the membership of the committee responsible for working on staffing.

_____ Action Item B: Analyze the effectiveness of your recent professional development program.

_____ Action Item C: Commit to developing and providing an ongoing, comprehensive professional development program.

_____ Action Item D: Set high standards for each inservice session.

_____ Action Item E: Change the ethic about professional development.

_____ Action Item F: Strategize, don't just prioritize.

_____ Action Item G: Acquire the best trainers available.

_____ Action Item H: Create "free" time for professional development.

_____ Action Item I: Include coaching.

_____ Action Item J: Involve your curriculum director.

6

The Inseparable Bodybrain Learning Partnership—Movement and Aerobic Exercise

One of life's truisms: The thing we're looking for is always in the last place we look. Isn't that a frustration! Well, having looked and looked for ways to improve our schools, perhaps here is that last place to look—the importance of movement and aerobic exercise to learning. Huge increases in student achievement are possible here, and with very little funding. No new staff, but professional development is essential.

$ Cutting Potential—0

Cost-Efficiency Ratio—10

The brain research couldn't be clearer or more conclusive—movement, especially aerobic exercise, builds the brain and significantly enhances learning.

MOVEMENT TO ENHANCE LEARNING

The Western world has long viewed the brain as rational, logical, ruler of all; the body in this scheme is merely the vehicle that carried the brain from one cerebral task to another. Exercise, dreaded by most, was simply an investment in beautification and/or stress reduction.

However, brain research reveals a markedly different story. Movement, and the more the better, actually grows the brain and significantly enhances its capacity to learn and perform. Conversely, lack of movement cripples the brain.

Mapping Your Future

Which school sounds most like yours?

- School A: inner-city elementary school, reduced incidents involving violence by nearly 60% in one year.
- School B: junior high in an economically depressed town, over a six-year period raised test scores from below the state average to 17% above in reading and 18% above in math; not a single fistfight among the 550 junior high students.
- School C: suburban school system, only 3% of a sophomore class were overweight; eighth graders, 97% of whom took the exam, scored sixth in math and first in science on the TIMSS (Trends in International Mathematics and Science Study) test.
- School District USA: one in three students are overweight or obese (a six-fold increase since 1990); test scores are disappointingly low; students are unmotivated; a high percentage of students are on medications for depression and/or hyperactivity; and violence levels are high and of increasing concern.

How do Schools A through C obtain such results?[1] They install a revolutionary physical education program based not in sports but on fitness—on leisure activities that can be pursued through adulthood. The program, called PE4Life, was pioneered by Phil Lawler, Naperville School District, near Chicago. It focuses on cardio-fitness as a lifestyle and thus provides and encourages a broad menu of options—from kayaking to dancing and rock climbing to typical sports played with fewer members (to keep everyone moving). Competitive sports are included but are not the focal point. Students are assessed on effort rather than skill or speed or strength.

The bottom line: A wide range of learning-enhancing effects on the brain can be achieved with daily doses of 35 minutes of aerobic activity that keep students' heart rates at 70% of their maximum plus brain-captivating doses of complexity.[2]

If you're like me, this information comes as a surprise—How could raising achievement scores and improving student behavior be so easy?

And with a groan—I hate exercising! And with a plea—please don't ask me to be a PE teacher!

But the facts stand squarely before us. Movement and aerobic exercise matter, and they matter a great deal. Lack of them affects everything else we do in the classroom.

The Benefits

For the Doubting Thomases (those who just don't believe it) and the Reluctant Sallies (those who believe it but are reluctant to act on it), here are three main benefits of a high-aerobics movement program of 35 minutes a day.[3] Such a program does the following:

- Kick-starts a leap in the growth of stem cells in the hippocampus (where new memories are formed)
- Produces significant increases in the chemicals the brain needs to spark attention and the physiological changes called learning (dendrite sprouting and connecting)
- Vastly improves most mental health conditions; particularly relevant for schools are depression, ADD, anxiety, and addiction

For more information about the effects of daily exercise on learning, see the resources section at the back of this chapter. Also, I strongly recommend you read *Spark: The Revolutionary New Science of Exercise and the Brain* by John J. Ratey, M.D. In addition to a description of the impact of exercise on learning, there are separate chapters on stress, anxiety, depression, attention deficit, addiction, hormonal changes, and aging. This is a must-read book for all stakeholders.

Cautionary note: Do understand that the potential for cutting budget in this area of program is likely zero for your school; however, this area holds the most potential for significantly improving student achievement and requires very little money.

From a parent perspective, a means of increasing achievement—or in a worst-case scenario, even offsetting the effects of budget turmoil—is a reason for real hope.

ACTION ITEMS

Action Item A: Create an Exercise and the Brain steering committee

Create an Exercise and the Brain steering committee composed of one teacher per grade level, the PE teacher, the school nurse, and other stakeholders. Schedule

> "... inactivity is killing our brains—physically shriveling them."
>
> —John J. Ratey, M.D.[4]

time to meet to help support and guide the grade-level teams. Complete the following tasks:

- If you don't have a PE specialist, select a member to become your resident expert on exercise and the brain. Arrange for the specialist or resident expert to visit a PE4Life school and attend a multiple-day training in PE4Life, *before* you begin your discussions for these action items.
- Ask your PTA to purchase a copy of *Spark: The Revolutionary New Science of Exercise and the Brain* for every teacher and additional copies for the school's professional library, available to all other stakeholders.
- Prepare to provide a book talk on *Spark* at an upcoming staff meeting.

Action Item B: Hijack a staff meeting

Provide a 20-minute (minimum) book-talk presentation of *Spark: The Revolutionary New Science of Exercise and the Brain.* Allow at least 15 to 20 minutes for follow-up questions and discussion. Present each staff member with a copy of *Spark.*

Action Item C: At a follow-up staff meeting, discuss the implications of implementing a PE4Life program

At a follow-up staff meeting, two to three weeks after the book talk, discuss the implications of implementing a PE4Life program for your students and school. Get agreement to proceed with fact finding.

Action Item D: Have the teacher members of the Exercise and the Brain steering committee interview their grade-level colleagues to collect baseline data classroom by classroom

Include at a minimum the following:

- Actual number of minutes a day students participate in physical exercise that keeps their pulse rate at least 70% of their maximum heart rate
- Percentage of students who are overweight and obese (Have your school nurse and/or PE teacher help gather this information.)
- Level of fitness (Collect what information is currently available, such as the President's Challenge Fitness test stats. If no data is available, that's your answer. If available, compile data for two or three years.)
- Average achievement scores for students who are overweight or obese versus those with normal body mass

- Number of students suffering from stress, anxiety, depression, attention deficit, and addiction (Ask the school nurse to provide these numbers by grade level, not classroom, so student privacy can be maintained.)
- Number of students with ADD and ADHD (Get this data from the nurse.)

Compile an average for each category by grade level. Note any trends that pop out from these numbers. Record this information on charts on PowerPoint slides so it can be readily shared.

Action Item E: Share each grade-level composite

Share each grade-level composite at the next staff meeting. Note any trends from grade level to grade level and within the school community as a whole. Compare your grade-level composites to state and national norms. Discuss what the data tells you. Record a summary of your discussions.

Action Item F: Meet by grade levels to brainstorm

Meet by grade levels to brainstorm at least three approaches to implement 35 minutes of daily aerobic activity in each classroom.

When looking for time, consider the following:

- The first 35 minutes of the current reading and/or language arts time slot three days of the week and of the current math time slot two days a week
- Transition times (from one subject to another, when mental states need to be reset such as following a long sustained period of work, coming back from assembly in the gym or from a study trip)
- The middle of any work period that is 90 minutes long
- A recess time that can be captured daily, or several times a week, and integrated into a 35-minute high-energy activity
- PE time that can be captured daily, or several times a week, and turned into a 35-minute high-energy activity
- Begin the school day 15 to 35 minutes earlier or add 15 to 35 minutes to the end of the day
- A combination of any of the above

When looking for content for these 35-minute, high-energy events, consider first and foremost movement to help students learn the curriculum content, such as the following:

- Bodymapping movements to represent concepts, words, or letters that help students learn content and skills (without or with music)[5]
- Student-generated movement routines to songs related to *being there* study trips (songs selected by students and approved by the teacher).

Consider the following to supplement regular aerobic exercises, especially for warm-up or cool-down:

- Dance routines, such as "YMCA" or "Macarena" or square dancing, hip-hop routines, line dancing, jitterbugging, dancing the Charleston, skip counting, and so on
- Commercial DVD workout routines, especially those with complex movements and/or rhythms
- Local marathons, walks, jogs, wellness celebrations, and so on[6]

Estimate the costs of each of the top three proposals, including staff development necessary to fully implement each approach.

Action Item G: Tasks of the Exercise and the Brain committee

- Review the work developed through Action Item F. Consolidate recommendations into a coherent plan. Present this plan, with timeline and budget, to the school community. Work toward consensus. Continue repeating the brainstorming under Action Item F and holding discussions with the school community until agreement on an action plan is reached.
- Once it is agreed where the 35 minutes a day can come from, request approval from the district office for such changes in schedule and/or policy.
- Assign each grade-level team the task of developing exercises that use subject area content so that each teacher doesn't have to do so on his or her own.
- Consider the following:
  - o Bodymapping routines created by students to help them remember information from subject area content
  - o High-energy simulations of concepts from science, social studies, and so on
  - o Games popular during the time period being studied
  - o Collecting such activities for use as Link Two curriculum content

- Create time for grade-level planning, preparation, and implementation. For example, assign all specialists to work with the same grade level at the same time—the music specialist works with one fourth-grade class while the art teacher works with another fourth-grade class, and another fourth-grade class goes to the computer lab, and so on. This frees up all fourth-grade teachers to work together—to plan, to prepare, and to receive movement training and coaching. (See scheduling options on pages 3.8–3.11.)
- Provide professional development—at least five hours of training per grade level, followed by at least two coaching sessions for each teacher (working one-on-one or by grade-level group). Bring in an expert in PE4Life.[7] Don't waste time reinventing the wheel.

- Create a process for periodically assessing implementation. Include questions such as the following:
  - Are we doing what we said we would do?
  - What is the impact on students—engagement, learning, and behavior—in the following conditions:
    - ★ In classrooms implementing as we planned?
    - ★ In classrooms with implementation that is consistent with the plan but infrequent?
    - ★ In classrooms with little or sporadic implementation and often not as planned?
    - ★ In classrooms that haven't begun implementing?
  - What are we learning?
  - What changes, if any, should we make?

Action Item H: Record the significant observations and decisions after every meeting

Assign two members of the group to record summaries of important discussions and all decisions. Be specific—what, when, who, how. Record on PowerPoint slides as well as on paper. Share this information at the beginning of every meeting to keep all stakeholders up to date.

RESOURCES

Brain Research Bits

Your handbook for this area of brain research is *Spark: The Revolutionary New Science of Exercise and the Brain* by John J. Ratey, M.D., with Eric Hagerman. Here are a few examples of the changes high aerobic exercise for 35 minutes daily can kick-start in the brain.

In the hippocampus.[8]

- Stimulates regenesis, the growth of new stem cells
- Spurs new stem cells to develop into new nerve cells
- Can cause a shrunken hippocampus (due to inactivity or aging) to return to normal size

These changes are crucial to learning because the hippocampus is where new memories are formed.

Production of chemicals to spark attention, learning, and long-term memory.

- Elevates brain-derived neurotrophic factor (BDNF), a protein that builds, protects, and maintains neuron circuitry, giving neurons the tools they need to learn—to process, associate, put in context, and remember.[9]

- BDNF is especially important in the formation of long-term memorics.
- Rate of learning is directly correlated with levels of BDNF. Levels rise as the amount of exercise increases.[10]
- In summary, BDNF gives the synapses the tools they need not only to take in information but also to process it, associate it, put it in context (with prior experiences and other elements in the current situation), and remember it.

Vastly improves most mental health conditions, particularly depression, anxiety, ADD, and addiction by stimulating the production of serotonin, norepinephrine, and dopamine and balancing them for optimum performance of the brain.[11]

- Serotonin helps keep brain activity under control by influencing mood, impulsivity, anger, and aggressiveness. (Note: Prozac is a serotonin substitute.)
- Norepinephrine amplifies brain signals that influence attention, perception, motivation, and arousal.
- Dopamine is thought of as the learning, reward (satisfaction), attention, and movement neurotransmitter. (Note: Ritalin is used to increase dopamine levels.)

According to John Ratey, "Voluntary exercise has a profound impact on cognitive abilities and mental health. It is simply one of the best treatments we have to most psychiatric problems."[12]

The amount of movement matters. The amount of exercise has a profound effect on the number of new stem cells that are formed.

The kind of movement matters. The more complex the movements, the more complex the synaptic connections. Aerobic exercise should also include new learning—acquisition of new physical skills and/or new mental skills and knowledge used for problem solving.

Academic results. Studies by the California Department of Education (CDE) have consistently shown that students with higher fitness scores also have higher test scores.[13]

- In 2002, fit kids scored twice as well on academic tests as their unfit peers.[14] Those fifth-, seventh-, and ninth-grade students passing all six portions of the fitness test significantly outranked their unfit peers. In reading, scores doubled from the 27th percentile to the 54th percentile; in math, the increase was from the 35th to the 68th percentile.[15] Even when socioeconomic status was factored in, the trend remained. And, among low-income students, fitter students scored better than unfit students.[16] Test results in 2004 were similar.

- Six areas of fitness were tested—aerobic capacity, percentage of body fat, abdominal strength and endurance, trunk strength and flexibility, upper body strength, and overall flexibility.[17] When researchers at the University of Illinois near Naperville replicated the CDE study, they found that two areas of the test were particularly important in relation to academic performance: increased aerobic fitness had a strong, positive relationship, and increased body mass had a strong, negative influence.[18]
- The researchers discovered that an electroencephalogram (EEG) showed more activity in fit kids' brains, indicating that more neurons were being recruited for the assigned tasks. Hillman also discovered that even a single, acute bout of exercise had a positive impact on learning. The formula goes something like this: aerobic exercise = faster cognitive processing speed = better attention (greater attentional control resulting in more accurate responses) = better learning.[19]
- In summary, physical activity has a positive influence on attention, concentration, memory, and classroom behavior. Clearly, fitness should not be looked upon as extracurricular but rather as a vital component in students' academic success.[20]

Despite such research, the increase in minutes for reading and math, in response to No Child Left Behind, has pulled the nation in the opposite direction. Many districts have cut or eliminated their PE programs. Some districts have even eliminated morning recess. Illinois, because of PE4Life, is now the only state that requires daily PE

MYTHS VERSUS BRAIN FACTS

Myths	Brain Facts
What's important is pushing yourself—no pain, no gain. And burn those calories! Exercise is about improving your appearance and self-confidence.	What's critical is the increase in oxygen and production of neurotransmitters, not how "fit" the person becomes. Working at 70% of one's aerobic capacity for 35 minutes a day is sufficient to create significant, learning-enhancing changes in the brain.
What's important is specializing and mastery (choose a sport and be a winner).	What's critical is enjoying what one is doing and adding novelty and/or complexity to the activities each session.

ENDNOTES

1. Perhaps the best-known fitness versus sports program is that pioneered by the Naperville School District near Chicago, Illinois, called PE4Life; it has fostered considerable research. Outcomes are impressive. For more information about the schools behind the thumbnail sketches here, see the Web sites for Woodland Elementary School, Kansas City, Missouri; Titusville Public Schools, Pennsylvania; and Naperville, respectively. Other useful sources of individual school test scores are GreatSchools.net or trulia.com. Also, see the discussion of this fitness-learning revolution in *Spark: The Revolutionary New Science of Exercise and the Brain* by John J. Ratey, M.D., with Eric Hagerman (New York: Little, Brown and Company, 2008). This is a pivotal book for educators wanting to improve student achievement despite declining budgets. Every staff member should have his or her own copy, and the school library should have several copies that parents can access.

2. Note that this time and pace—35 minutes daily—is the minimum necessary to spark the brain responses described here; time for dressing, showering, getting organized, cooling down, and so on, is *not* included in this 35 minutes. Also, complexity and challenge matter. Complexity refers to activities that challenge the bodybrain partnership such as novel (to the learner) movements or music with an unusual beat, and most important of all, immediate post-exercise challenge, such as reading in a subject area that is a stretch for the learner, crossword puzzles, problem solving of any kind, novel experiences, and so on. In schools, an optimum scenario would be aerobics just prior to a student's most difficult subject.

3. These effects of aerobic exercise, based on numerous studies over the past decade, have been widely reported and are also generally accepted science. For a user-friendly summary, see "The Effects of Exercise on the Brain," www.serendip .brynmawr.edu/bb/neuro/neuro05/web2/mmcgovern.html.

4. Ratey, *Spark*, 4. The lethal nature of inactivity has been known for more than 20 years; see the work of enrichment theory pioneer Marian Diamond in *Magic Trees of the Mind: How to Nurture Your Child's Intelligence, Creativity, and Healthy Emotions From Birth Through Adolescence* (New York: Penguin, 1998). "Use it or lose it" is a solid brain research fact.

5. Bodymapping is using body movements to represent words, concepts, and symbols to facilitate learning skills and content. There are dozens of sources for bodymapping, including *Minds in Motion: A Kinesthetic Approach to Teaching Elementary Curriculum* (Portsmouth, NH: Heinemann, 1998), by Susan Griss, that demonstrate how to teach skills and content through movement. Also, see the work of Jean Bladyes-Madigan, *Action-Based Learning*, at www.actionbasedlearning.com.

6. To find local events, see Web sites such as www.nationalwellness.org/; americanheart.org/presenter.jhtml?identifier=2360; and saferoutestoschools.org/ walk/.

7. To locate a PE4Life training opportunity, see www.pe4life.org/.

8. This area of research is well established. For one of many surveys, see "The Effects of Exercise on the Brain" by M. K. McGovern, serendip.brynmawr .edu/bb/neuro/neuro05/web2/mmcgovern.html.

9. Numerous studies have explored the role of BDNF in learning; they overlap and confirm. For more information, see Carl W. Cotman, *Activity Dependent Plasticity in the Aging Brain*, University of California Irvine, 2004. For a brief, user-friendly overview, also see M. K. McGovern, "Effects of Exercise on the Brain."

10. It is important to note that there is a point beyond which increased aerobic exercise does not continue to increase BDNF. However, few push their exercise regimen beyond this point. And certainly, 35 minutes daily comes nowhere close to reaching this plateau.

11. See M. K. McGovern, "Effects of Exercise on the Brain," for a reader-friendly summary (serendip.brynmawr.edu/bb/neuro/neuro05/web2/mmcgovern.html).

12. Ratey, *Spark*, 7.

13. According to Jim Grissom, although "the overall health benefits of organized physical activity are probably much more important than possible academic benefits . . . when policy makers need to make difficult decisions about where to spend public funds and administrators need to make decisions about where to focus resources in a climate of academic accountability, a proven relationship between physical fitness and academic achievement could be used as an argument to support, retain, and perhaps even improve physical education programs." "Physical Fitness and Academic Achievement" (*Journal of Exercise PhysiologyOnline* (JEPonline), 8 (no. 1, February 2005): 12.

14. See the summary, "California Physical Fitness Test: A Study of the Relationship Between Physical Fitness and Academic Achievement in California Using 2004 Test Results" by Jim Grissom (California State Department of Education, 2004). For a more academic discussion, see "Physical Fitness and Academic Achievement," *Journal of Exercise PhysiologyOnline* (JEPonline), 8 (no. 1, February 2005).

15. Grissom, "Physical Fitness and Academic Achievement." Stanford Achievement Test: 9 mean curve equivalent increases were from 42 to 60 (roughly a 33 percentile increase) in reading and a 37 to 52 MCE increase (24 percentile increase) in math. See page 16.

16. Grissom, CDE study, 5–6.

17. The CDE physical fitness test, called the Fitnessgram, was developed by the Cooper Institute for Aerobics Research in Dallas, Texas. Included in the CDE study were 371,198 fifth graders, 366,278 seventh graders, and 298,910 ninth graders.

18. Darla Castelli, C. H. Hillman, S. M. Buck, and H. E. Erwin, "Physical Fitness and Academic Achievement in Third- and Fifth-Grade Students," *Journal of Sport & Exercise Psychology*, 29 (2007), 239–252.

19. See C. H. Hillman, M. B. Pontiflex, L. B. Raine, D. M. Castelli, E. E. Hall, and A. F. Kramer, "The Effect of Acute Treadmill Walking on Cognitive Control and Academic Achievement in Preadolescent Children," *Neuroscience* 159 (2009), 1044–1064. In preadolescents, a single acute bout of moderately intense aerobic exercise improves cognitive performance in reading and increases response accuracy (improved cognitive control). According to the researchers, acute exercise might serve as a cost-effective means for improving specific aspects of academic achievement and enhancing cognitive control during preadolescence (1059–1060).

Hillman also found that in adults, single bouts of exercise may increase attentional resource allocation and improve cognitive processing speed (from a 2003 study reported in the above 2009 article, page 1046). In schools, what's good for the goose is also good for the gander. Staff and parent volunteers should explore the benefits of becoming fit and consider becoming role models.

20. Conversation July 13, 2009, with Jim Grissom, Ph.D. Research and Evaluation Consultant, Standards & Assessment Division, California Department of Education.

ACTION SUMMARY CHECKLIST

_____ Action Item A: Create an Exercise and the Brain steering committee:

- Select a member to become your resident expert on exercise and the brain. Arrange for him or her to visit a PE4life school and attend training.
- Ask your PTA to purchase a copy of *Spark* for every teacher and the school's professional library, available to other stakeholders.
- Prepare to provide a book talk on *Spark* at an upcoming staff meeting.

_____ Action Item B: Hijack a staff meeting.

_____ Action Item C: At a follow-up staff meeting, discuss the implications of implementing a PE4Life program.

_____ Action Item D: Have the teacher members of the Exercise and the Brain steering committee interview their grade-level colleagues to collect baseline data classroom by classroom.

_____ Action Item E: Share each grade-level composite at the next staff meeting.

_____ Action Item F: Meet by grade levels to brainstorm at least three approaches to implementing 35 minutes of daily aerobic activity.

_____ Action Item G: Tasks of the Exercise and the Brain committee:

- Review the work developed through Action Item F. Consolidate recommendations into a coherent plan.
- Request approval from the district office for such changes in schedule and policy.

- Assign each grade-level team the task of developing exercises that use subject area content so that each teacher doesn't have to reinvent the wheel on his or her own.
- Create time for grade-level planning, preparation, and implementation.
- Provide professional development—at least five hours of training per grade level, followed by at least two coaching sessions for each teacher.
- Create a process for periodically assessing implementation.
- Assign two group members to record summaries of important discussions and decisions. Be specific—what, when, who, how.

_____ Action Item H: Record the significant observations and decisions after every meeting—Assign two members of the group to record summaries of important discussions and all decisions.

The Inseparable Bodybrain Learning Partnership—Emotion

Mounds of studies about emotion have accumulated over the past 30 years. But perhaps the best summary is this by Dr. Robert Sylwester:[1]

"Emotion drives attention, which
drives learning,
memory,
problem solving, and
just about everything else."

IMPACT OF EMOTION AS GATEKEEPER TO LEARNING AND PERFORMANCE

The term *gatekeeper* does not overstate the power of emotion. It is central to the brain's processing—from perceiving, to processing, to formulating a response.

$ Cutting Potential—1

Cost-Efficiency Ratio—8

Here are some important points:

Because we humans are social animals, the emotional climate in the classroom flows from the quality of student-student and teacher-student relationships.

Implications: A sense of community matters. Students who feel like outsiders have nothing to lose and no incentive to contribute.

"An emotionally charged event is the best processed kind of external stimulus ever measured." Such events persist much longer in our memories and are recalled with greater accuracy than neutral memories.[2]

Implications: Boredom is deadly, a black hole during the learning process. So is frustration.

"The more attention the brain pays to a given stimulus, the more elaborately the information will be encoded and retained." In other words, "better attention always equals better learning. It improves retention of reading materials and accuracy and clarity in writing, math, and science" (and probably every other academic category, but these three are the only ones tested so far).[3] Why? Because when the brain detects an emotionally charged event, the amygdala releases dopamine into the system (dopamine greatly aids memory and information processing).[4]

Implication: Learning via all or most of the 19 senses, such as at a *being there* experience, provides the perfect interplay between complexity of sensory input and high emotional engagement. Textbooks, worksheets, and lectures are low in sensory input and thus shut the gate on learning and performance.

Learning via the electrical-chemical system of neurons, dendrites, axons, and synapses—which has been known for decades—is but one means by which neurons receive and process information. A second biological system, discovered in the 1990s largely through the work of Candace Pert,[5] is a wholly chemical system of learning. Proteins—neurotransmitters, peptides, hormones, factors, and protein ligands, collectively referred to as "information substances"—are produced and received through receptors on the cell membrane. All are received by the brain, and many are also received, and produced, throughout the body. Pert calls these the "molecules of emotion." This bodybrain communication is the basis for the description of learning as an inseparable bodybrain partnership. In the words of John Ratey, physician and author of numerous books about the brain, "We are learning that emotions are the rules of multiple brain and body systems that are distributed over the whole person. We cannot separate emotion from cognition or cognition from the body."[6]

Implication: Like Doublemint gum, optimum learning occurs when the two parallel learning systems are activated together.

Necessary Components of an Environment
That Enhances the Role of Emotion as Gatekeeper

Classroom components of an environment that enhances the impact of emotion on learning and performance include the following:[7]

- Positive relationships—student to student and teacher to student
- A sense of community, in the classroom and schoolwide
- Absence of threat (Note: Threat is in the eye of the beholder; absence of threat means lack of perceived threat. However, this does not mean absence of appropriate consequences.)
- A physical environment that is safe, clean, healthful,[8] and pleasant
- A learning environment with challenge that motivates but doesn't create excessive anxiety or a sense of futility, and that also nurtures reflective thinking
- Curriculum that is conceptual and provides practice in using content and skills in meaningful (to the learner) ways
- Instructional practices that engage students, carry them through the Two-Step Learning process, and empower them through social/political action and service projects

For more information about creating an environment that enhances the role of emotion as gatekeeper to learning and performance, see *Exceeding Expectations: A User's Guide to Implementing Brain Research in the Classroom*, 4th ed., Chapters 8 through 10.

ACTION ITEMS

Action Item A: Create a work committee

Create a work committee composed of one teacher per grade level plus other stakeholders. Design an emotional climate assessment instrument, such as that in Figure 7A on page 7.4, and a process for administering it. (For thoughts on developing an assessment process, see Resources, pages 7.7–7.8.)

Action Item B: Complete an emotional climate assessment

To complete an emotional climate assessment such as the one that follows, each grade-level teacher must take responsibility for his or her grade level—providing leadership for the task, for ensuring that the emotional climate assessments are completed, and for presenting the findings to the entire staff.

Action Item C: Study the climate assessments

Consider such questions as the following:

- Are the responses—a student's, his or her parent's, and teacher's—in agreement? If not, why?

Emotional Climate Assessment

Classroom Code #		**Participant Code #**

1   Rating Scale   **5**

Absence of Threat

Student to student—
-No sense of community—
social environment run by
cliques and in-groups
-Not safe—bullying, not belonging
_____

Student to student—
-Sense of belonging—safe
to hold differing opinions
and to disagree
-Respect for others and self
_____

-Fear of ridicule (dummy, geek)

-Confidence in ability to
learn; knows how to direct
own learning

Teacher to student—
-Fear of bad grades, ridicule,
being embarrassed, being
labeled
-No relationship with teacher—
nothing to lose by misbehaving
_____

Teacher to student—
-In relationship with teacher,
mutual respect, trust, and
affinity
-Social environment under
leadership of the teacher
_____

-Bored

-Curious, eager to learn

Engagement

-Must be prodded to do tasks
-Doesn't volunteer to participate
in class or in Learning Clubs
_____

-Sticks with tasks until
completed; high level of
workmanship
_____

-Homework almost always a
source of conflict at home

-Self-starter, looks forward
to learning challenges

-Reactive, attention scattered

-Focused on learning

Nurturing Reflective Thinking

-Doesn't expect classroom
work to apply to his or her life
-Difficulty working on own
_____

-Seeks ways to use concepts
and skills in own life in realworld
settings
-Works well on own
_____

-Doesn't spend time thinking
about "why" or "what if"
questions

-Spends time thinking about
"why" questions

Average Score

0 **MILES**	25	50	75	100

For every 25 miles driven on this road trip, expect a 5+ percentile increase in student achievement.

Remember: "Emotion drives attention, which drives learning, memory, problem solving, and just about everything else."

Figure 7A

- Are the student and parent responses consistent within a classroom, or are there significant differences among students? If there are differences, are there patterns, for example, highest to lowest achieving students, ESL to native English speakers, higher to lower income, and so on? What are the reasons for these differences?
- Does the average of student and parent responses from a classroom equal the composite completed by that teacher?
- What are the strengths and weaknesses of our program in providing an emotional environment that enhances learning?
- Taking a step back, what have we learned from this process?

Record your findings on charts or PowerPoint slides to be shared with others.

Action Item D: Determine need for reinvestment in this area

To determine the need to reinvest in this area, consider the following interpretation of your ratings:

Rating	The emotional climate is having a . . .
1–2	Severely negative impact on student achievement levels. Make reinvestment and improvement work here our first professional priority.
2–3	Very negative impact on student achievement. Reinvest money before we address instructional tools and curriculum.
3–4	Capping effect on student achievement. It is unlikely we'll be able to improve achievement (except through movement and aerobic exercise) until the emotional climate is more supportive. However, work on this area should be combined with work on improving instructional tools and curriculum, especially for Step Two.
4–5	Positive effect on learning—a strength in our program.

Develop priorities. What area(s) is most critical to address first versus where is the best starting point strategically? Prepare charts or PowerPoint slides to accompany your presentation to the entire staff. Have each grade-level group discuss the findings and recommendations presented. After 15 minutes, have each group record their responses and post on the wall. Using a Gallery Walk, have each group read the responses of the other groups. Return to your group and make your final decisions about the recommendations. Report to the group as a whole. If there are significant areas of disagreement, have the steering committee take the recommendations under advisement and come back to the group with final recommendations.

Action Item E: Involve your district office and school board

Invite a staff member from the district office and a member of the school board to sit in during a meeting of one of the grade-level work committees as they interpret their findings and compile their report and recommendations for presentation to the school community. Understanding the process that results in program recommendations helps policy makers make better decisions, including providing the needed support for implementation.

Action Item F: Present your findings and recommendations to the school community

After the presentation, have each group (those at a table or in groups of 4–6 people) discuss the findings and recommendations presented. After 10 to 15 minutes, have each group record their responses on Post-its and post them on the wall on butcher paper labeled with the categories presented.

Using a gallery walk, have each group read the responses of the other groups. Return to your group and, working toward consensus, make your final decisions about the recommendations. Report to the group as a whole.

If there are significant areas of disagreement, have the grade-level work committees and steering committee consider the recommendations and come back to the group with final recommendations.

Action Item G: Finalize your decisions, including actions to be taken and a budget for professional development

Establish a timeline by which elements of a supportive emotional environment will be completed. For example,

Year One	• Physical environment (safe, clean, healthful, and pleasant)[9] • Positive relationships and sense of community[10] • Absence of threat[11]
Year Two	• A learning environment with challenge that motivates but doesn't create excessive anxiety or a sense of futility[12] • Instructional practices that engage students through the 19 senses, carry them through the Two-Step Learning process, and empower them through social/political action and service projects[13]
Year Three	• Curriculum that is conceptual and provides practice in using content and skills in meaningful (to the learner) ways[14]

Action Item H: Create an ongoing assessment process

Create an ongoing assessment process that will provide annual feedback on your progress. Include behavior incident reports (frequency and severity), attendance figures, book checkout at the library (especially nonfiction), a repeat of your emotional climate assessment, a comparison of test scores, and other indicators you think will help tell the story.

RESOURCES

Two resources are included as follows:

- Thoughts on creating an assessment process
- Sources for further study

Thoughts on Developing an Assessment Process

To ensure reliable information without making data collection an overwhelming task, consider the following:

- Using a random numbers table, select 30% of the students in each classroom. Schedule the student and his or her parent for an interview.
- Recruit sociology students from a nearby college, student teachers, parents, or community members. Provide a mini-training on interviewing techniques and how to use the Emotional Assessment form. Include real or simulated interviews so that trainees learn to calibrate their responses; calibration of the nine scores recorded in the bubbles on the survey (and the average) will make the scores across grade levels reliable and thus informative.
- If possible, have the same interviewer do all the interviews for a classroom.
- Have the interviewer fill out an Emotional Climate Assessment form for each interview. Identify the forms by numbers, not names; for example, S1 for the student and P1 for that student's parent, S2 and P2, for each classroom, and so on.
- Have the classroom teacher complete the form for each of the identified students, using the same numbering system so that the three points of view (student, parent, and teacher) can be pulled together for each student without violating the student's privacy.
- Also, consider assessing the emotional climate teacher to teacher and teachers to administrators. With minor tweaking, the Emotional Climate Assessment in Figure 7A on page 7.4 could serve as a base for such assessment. Or a more straightforward approach would be to attach a one-through-five scale (one being low and five being high) to each of the Lifelong Guidelines.[15] Teachers would complete this survey twice: once rating the teacher-to-teacher emotional climate and once rating the teacher-to-administrator emotional climate.

For example, see the following:

Emotional Work Climate—Teacher to Teacher

As a teacher, this is how I rate the teacher-to-teacher emotional work climate on the following dimensions (1 is low; 5 is high):

_____   Trustworthiness—Are worthy of my trust and confidence

_____   Truthfulness—Act with personal responsibility and mental accountability at all times

_____   Active Listening—Listen attentively and with the intention of understanding what I'm intending to convey

_____   No Put-Downs—Never use words, actions, and/or body language that degrade, humiliate, or dishonor me

_____   Personal Best—Do their best for team efforts and commitments given the circumstances and available resources

---

Emotional Work Climate—Teacher to Administrator

As a teacher, this is how I rate the teacher-to-administrator emotional work climate (1 is low; 5 is high):

_____   Trustworthiness—Are worthy of my trust and confidence

_____   Truthfulness—Act with personal responsibility and mental accountability; each trusts the other to always speak the truth

_____   Active Listening—Listen attentively and with the intention of understanding me

_____   No Put-Downs—Never use words, actions, and/or body language that degrade, humiliate, or dishonor me

_____   Personal Best—Do their best for team efforts and commitments given the circumstances and available resources

---

Administrators should complete the above survey as well.

Sources for Further Study

- *Exceeding Expectations: A User's Guide to Implementing Brain Research in the Classroom,* 4th ed., Chapter 2 (vol. 1), Chapters 6 through 11 (vol. 2), and Chapters 12 through 15 (vol. 3).
- *Reaching All by Creating TRIBES Learning Communities* by Jeanne Gibbs (Windsor, CA: CenterSource Systems, 2006).

ENDNOTES

1. Dr. Robert Sylwester, Professor Emeritus, University of Oregon, has been a tireless translator of brain research for educators for three decades. Through his books and a busy speaking schedule, he has made the technical field of brain research accessible and understandable to thousands. This quote is typical of his ability to synthesize a great deal of information and make it not only understandable but memorable. Dr. Sylwester's recent books include *The Adolescent Brain: Reaching for Autonomy* (2007) and *How to Explain a Brain: An Educator's Handbook of Brain Terms and Cognitive Processes* (2005). He also writes a monthly column for the Internet journal *Brain Connection* (www.brainconnection.com).

2. Medina, John, *Brain Rules: 12 Principles for Surviving and Thriving at Work, Home, and School* (Seattle, WA: Pear Press, 2008), 80.

3. Medina, 74.

4. Medina, 80–81.

5. Dr. Candace Pert was the first to discover the chemical components of emotion. Her autobiographical account of her research, *Molecules of Emotion: Why You Feel the Way You Feel,* is a fascinating read both for the science and as an autobiography. In later editions of her book, she changed the subtitle to "The Scientific Basis Behind Mind-Body Medicine."

6. John J. Ratey, M.D. *A User's Guide to the Brain: Perception, Attention, and the Four Theaters of the Brain* (New York: Pantheon Books, 2001), 223.

7. These elements are building blocks of an emotional environment that enhances learning. The first four are considered prerequisites and must be addressed before and during the first year. See *Exceeding Expectations: A User's Guide to Implementing Brain Research in the Classroom,* 4th ed., by Susan J. Kovalik and Karen D. Olsen (Federal Way, WA: The Center for Effective Learning, 2009).

8. *The Healthy School Handbook: Conquering the Sick Building Syndrome and Other Environmental Hazards in and Around Your School,* edited by Norma Miller, is a powerful and convenient resource for analyzing the health of your school building and grounds and what impact unhealthy environments have on learning. This is a must-read book for those responsible for the maintenance, repairs, and remodeling of your school. A video of the same title is also available. If the rate of ADD/ADHD students at your school seems unusually high, be aware that there are a number of neurotoxins whose symptoms mimic ADD. Finding and eliminating such toxins will bring an immediate change in behavior for these "canary" students and staff, those significantly more sensitive to such environmental factors. Published by NEA Professional Library, Washington, DC, 1995.

9. As you plan to improve the physical environment, see *Exceeding Expectations: A User's Guide to Implementing Brain Research in the Classroom,* 4th ed., by Susan J. Kovalik and Karen D. Olsen (2009), Chapter 6, 6.3–20 (vol. 2).

10. For more information about creating positive relationships and a sense of community that enhances academic performance, see *Exceeding Expectations,* Chapter 7, 7.4–16, and Chapters 8 and 9 (vol. 2).

11. For more information about ensuring absence of threat, see *Exceeding Expectations,* Chapter 7, 7.4–8 and 7.13–17, and Chapter 11 (vol. 2).

12. For more information about creating and sustaining a learning environment with challenge that motivates, see *Exceeding Expectations,* Chapter 9, 9.1–9 (vol. 2).

13. For more information about instructional strategies that engage the 19 senses and carry students through Two-Step Learning, see *Exceeding Expectations*, Chapter 12 (vol. 3).

14. For more information about developing a conceptual curriculum, see *Exceeding Expectations*, Chapters 13–17 (vol. 3).

15. The Lifelong Guidelines, and the LIFESKILLS that define Personal Best, are the basis for classroom leadership and management in the *HET* (Highly Effective Teaching) model. Although developed for student use in the classroom, they are also the core of the agreed-upon behaviors adopted by staff and the basis for creating a sense of community and school as a place for learning. Their definitions are somewhat modified here for this survey form.

For more information, see *Exceeding Expectations*, Chapters 7, 8, and 9.

ACTION SUMMARY CHECKLIST

_____ Action Item A: Create a work committee:
- Design an emotional climate assessment instrument.
- Develop a process for administering it.

_____ Action Item B: Complete an emotional climate assessment.

_____ Action Item C: Study the climate assessments—Record your findings on charts or PowerPoint slides to be shared with others.

_____ Action Item D: Determine need for reinvestment in this area.

_____ Action Item E: Involve your district office and school board.

_____ Action Item F: Present your findings and recommendations to the school community.

_____ Action Item G: Finalize your decisions, including actions to be taken and a budget for professional development—Establish a timeline.

_____ Action Item H: Create an ongoing assessment process.

8

Double-Link Curriculum for Two-Step Learning— Link One

For the record, curriculum is not an area with high potential for budget cutting (unless, of course, your school pays an annual fee for a commercial curriculum program). And it's an expensive, very time-

<table>
<tr><td>$ Cutting Potential—2</td></tr>
<tr><td>Cost-Efficiency Ratio—7</td></tr>
</table>

consuming[1] realm to improve. However, if your school has already made substantial progress cutting budget and improving your program as outlined in Chapters 2 through 7 and 10, making improvements in curriculum will pay off handsomely. *Until then, place curriculum on the back burner.*

A CONTEXT FOR CONTENT

To begin our discussion of curriculum, let's use a communications example. When communicating, *how* you say *what* you say can get you in trouble. But no amount of spin on *how* you say something can overcome a bad *what*. Likewise, poor instructional processes can neutralize good curriculum, but the best instructional strategies come to naught if the curriculum isn't designed with Two-Step Learning in mind. (See the discussion of Two-Step Learning in Chapter 3, page 3.2, and in Appendices A and B.)

So, when students are not learning, despite your best efforts to improve instruction, look at your curriculum. Once it's designed with Two-Step Learning and age appropriateness in mind, revisit your instructional tools and ensure that you provide sufficient professional development in the instructional strategies to ensure delivery of Double-Link curriculum described in this and the next chapter.

Two Links of a Chain

As you examine your curriculum, think of it in terms of two links of a chain. *The first link* is the content needed for Step One of Learning[2]— pattern seeking and making meaning. This content consists of the statements of what is to be learned—the concepts and the significant knowledge and skills needed to understand and apply the concepts. To enhance students' ability to perceive pattern, content should be stated as conceptually as possible and skills should be stated exactly as you want students to remember them. These statements are your school's version of your state's curriculum standards.

Examples of Conceptual Curriculum

- The physical characteristics of animals and plants vary greatly and determine what they can do and how they do it in order to meet their needs (form and function). (second grade)
- The function or use of something is usually related to its shape. (second grade)
- All things change over time. (third grade)
- Interactions to meet the need for food within a habitat are called a food chain or more accurately, a food web. The disappearance of just one animal or plant can cause a food web to collapse and members of the web to die out. (fourth grade)
- Machines make work easier. Machines and other forms of technology extend the ability of people to change the world: to cut, shape, or put together materials; to move things from one place to another; and to reach farther with their hands, voices, senses, and minds. Such changes may be for survival needs (such as food, shelter, and defense), for communication and transportation, to gain and share knowledge and express ideas, or to satisfy a market need and thus make money. (fourth grade)
- A system is a collection of things and processes (and often people) that interact to perform some function. (fifth grade)
- A system is usually connected to other systems, both internally and externally. Thus, a system may be thought of as containing

subsystems and as being a subsystem of a larger system (for example, all the systems within a city or town that are essential to the existence of the city, such as transportation, water, garbage, sewer, hospital, police, and fire; other examples include the human body, ecosystems, human-made habitats such as a shopping mall, school and regional transportation systems, communes, and Biosphere 2 [and similar attempts at creating self-sustaining environments]). (sixth grade)

- A change in one system may disrupt all the other interrelated systems. (sixth grade)

Examples of Skills

- There are a variety of ways to record and display data in order to make the information easier to interpret. Always use the form of graph that would best assist the reader to interpret the data. Some examples of graphs and graphic organizers include bar, line, circle, pie, and axis graphs, simple columns, Venn diagrams, and mindmaps.

  o Bar and line graphs are used to compare two pieces of data on a grid.
  o Circle and pie graphs assist in visually displaying how several pieces of something create a whole.
  o Axis graphs assist in observing directions or trends or how much of two ingredients must be increased or decreased in order to reach a desired goal.
  o Column charts simply separate the data by designated characteristics; (examples include bookkeeping formats, decision-making formats such plus, minus, or neutral (P, M, –) effects, and so forth.
  o Venn diagrams assist the observer in comparing two entities for differences and similarities.
  o Mindmaps can present a large amount of data and, most important, show the interrelationships among the data or elements. Since a mindmap is a visual format, it gives the brain more clues for analyzing relationships and remembering the big idea and its relevant details.

- Scientists use a standard called a quadrat to observe, compare, and study living and nonliving things. A quadrat has specific dimensions and can be set up in different ways using different materials, such as rope, string, coat hangers bent into squares, small twigs, or sticks. Once the quadrat has been established, observation must be restricted to the area within the quadrat. As the data is collected, notes are taken to aid accurate and comprehensive recall at a later date.

For practical advice on how to develop content for Link-One curriculum, called key points, see *Exceeding Expectations: A User's Guide to*

Implementing Brain Research in the Classroom, 4th ed., Chapters 12 and 16 and pages 13.4–8 (vol. 3).

The second link, addressed in Chapter 9, is the content needed for Step Two of learning. Link-Two curriculum should propel learning through developing programs to use what is understood and wire it into long-term memory. This content consists of activities for using what is understood in real-world situations—the kinds of situations that students have already had experience with and those they see people around them facing on a daily basis.

For practical advice on how to develop content for Link-Two curriculum, known as inquiries, see *Exceeding Expectations: A User's Guide to Implementing Brain Research in the Classroom,* Chapters 12 and 17, pages 13.9–16, and sample curriculum in Chapter 14 (vol. 3).

Examples of Double-Link Curriculum for Two-Step Learning

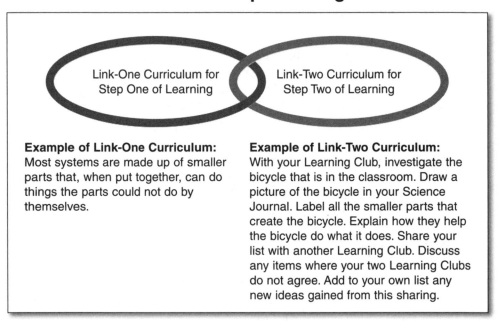

Figure 8A

CONTENT FOR LINK-ONE CURRICULUM

Think of curriculum development for Link One as a pattern-enhancing activity. By that I mean that the more readily curriculum content enables students to detect and make meaning of patterns (Step One of learning), the more readily students can create meaning and thus the more powerful and efficient your curriculum.

Powerful Link-One curriculum meets three criteria:[3]

- Generalizable—it can be used to explain details. If one understands a concept, supporting details are easily understandable. This eliminates the need to memorize. As Frank Smith has noted, "Understanding takes care of learning."[4]
- Transferable to new locations or situations. In other words, instead of having to start from scratch in each learning situation, transferable content allows students to quickly understand a great deal about a new situation and/or location. This significantly speeds up learning and strengthens wiring into long-term memory. This saves instructional time and improves learning.
- Age appropriate.

For a deeper understanding of pattern seeking needed to analyze your curriculum, see Appendix A.

Generalizable and Transferable = Conceptual

Generalizable and transferable patterns are concepts. For example, after learning about the concept of parasitism or predator-prey relationships in biology, students can apply it to economics, such as behavior of huge multinational corporations, predatory lending by banks, or the playground bully extorting lunch money from younger students, or see the contrast with symbiosis and small, community-oriented businesses. Or if students understand the concept of habitat in a desert environment, they can quickly anticipate and piece together major elements in a rain forest habitat.

Link-One curriculum must be stated as conceptually as possible.

The opposite of conceptual curriculum is curriculum filled with factoids—fragments that have no meaning. They are the dates of history that, by themselves, are meaningless. They are the definitions of words that are isolated and without connection to prior experience or meaningful wholes. They are the dreaded stuff students must memorize because they are meaningless and thus make pattern seeking impossible. They therefore leave the brain with no other strategy to employ but memorization, for example, fourteen hundred and ninety-two, Columbus sailed the ocean blue; $E = mc^2$ (unless you're a physics whiz graduate student), and countless other statements lacking a sense of why or to what end or even an understanding of what is.

In summary: In the world of our biological brain, patterns are neural food. They are what our brain seeks and that from which it extracts meaning. Concepts are rich, powerful patterns for the brain, useful in unlocking meaning around us and more easily stored in long-term memory than curriculum fragments and factoids. To learn fragments and factoids, students mostly resort to memorization; in contrast, concepts allow students to leapfrog from today's lesson to yesterday's personal experience to tomorrow's situations in life.

Also, concepts travel. They don't stay where we last put them, such as in science or art. They know no curriculum borders. They are not stopped by time or space. That's why they are so good at integrating curriculum. And when we integrate curriculum, and thus study two or more subjects simultaneously, we can then double the hours in our day. (For more examples of Link One, see pages 8.12–8.14.)

Age Appropriateness

Over the past 20 years, the political push to raise standards, however well intended, has had some unfortunate side effects. Chief among them has been demanding curriculum content that is beyond the unfolding developmental level of the students' brain at each grade level. Currently, every subject area has age-inappropriate content. Examples from science curriculum include the following:

- First Grade: atoms and molecules, landforms around the world
- Second Grade: climate changes creating extinction, light waves
- Third Grade: photosynthesis, particles in matter, energy: work, weather changes due to tilting of the earth on its axis
- Fourth Grade: heat as particle activity
- Fifth Grade: atoms, elements, compounds, nuclear fusion (much of the traditional content for fifth grade should be moved to junior and senior high)
- Sixth Grade: almost all areas of traditional content for sixth grade should be moved to high school

The pragmatic test for age-appropriate content is this: *If, after teaching and reteaching something with full sensory input, students still cannot understand the concept, then it is age inappropriate* for students at that grade level.[5]

All age-inappropriate content should be eliminated from the curriculum by doing the following:

- Pushing it upward to an appropriate age level (typically to junior or senior high school)
- Pushing it to the end of the year to join content that is never reached before the year runs out (a process called "selective abandonment")
- Deleting it altogether

If politics demands it stay, wrap it up in with a familiar tune or build it into a rap and have students memorize it as a fun musical-dance experience. But don't waste time slavishly trying to teach it.[6]

When content is beyond what students can understand at their stage of brain development, their only recourse is to drop out, act out, or resort to memorizing for a test, which evaporates from short-term memory within hours of the quiz. This frustrates students and teachers and wastes time and money. Worse, it convinces students they hate that subject; worse yet, students become convinced that they must be "dumb."

Another unfortunate side effect of the stampede to raise standards was an increase in expectations for the *quantity* of what students must learn. In turn, this increased pressure on teachers to "cover" even more material, virtually guaranteeing that time would be insufficient to wire yet more content into long-term memory.

Although budget-cutting opportunities here are slim to zero, decisions to eliminate age-inappropriate content can significantly improve students' attitude about a subject and significantly improve students' understanding of what they're trying to learn. It also give teachers the gift of time.

See Appendix C for a discussion of age appropriateness and the thinking capabilities of children at each grade level, K–6.

ACTION TASK 1: ANALYZE YOUR CURRICULUM FOR AGE APPROPRIATENESS

Action Item A: Tasks for the steering committee

Tasks for the steering committee (likely the same committee of stakeholders assembled for Action Item A, page 1.4):

- Select the subject area to begin with. (Select the second area only *after* you've completed work on the first. The learning curve here will be steep and the consequences of your decisions will be far-reaching.) *Recommendation:* Leave the basic skills until last.
- Aim for consensus.
- Train several teachers, preferably one per grade level, to become expert in age-appropriate learning.
- Create a chart like the one in Figure 8B on page 8.8 to be used by each grade-level committee. List all curriculum standards for every grade level in the first column. (This could be done by a parent volunteer.)

Analysis of Age Appropriateness

Grade Level _____ Curriculum Standard	Age Appropriate yes/no	Recommended Action 1 2 3
•		
•		
•		

Legend for Recommended Action: 1 = Push up to ___X___ grade level at your school

2 = Delete from your school's curriculum

3 = Push to end of year ("selective abandonment")

Figure 8B

Selective abandonment[7] is a term for moving content to the end of the year with full knowledge that no teacher can ever cover everything in every subject. Effectively, this means that the content will not be addressed and, in fact, isn't intended to be. Although it may not be the most courageous or noble recourse, it's a practical solution to a volatile political issue. Putting age-appropriate curriculum first will buy time for teachers to teach more content through both steps of Two-Step Learning.

Action Item B: Tasks for grade-level teams

Involve every classroom teacher in this action item if possible. Understanding the importance of age appropriateness will be crucial for full and accurate implementation. Also, include parents and other community stakeholders; their understanding and support are critical. Tasks for each grade-level work group include the following:

- Begin with an overview of how the brain grows through developmental stages; answer any questions about the information and the research behind it and then work through the curriculum for that grade level.
- As a committee, comb through your curriculum, comparing each standard to the description of age-appropriate content in Appendix C. If you determine a standard is age inappropriate, be sure to complete the last column, giving your recommendation for dealing with it. Use the expertise of your work group's resident expert on age appropriateness.

- Aim for consensus. If agreement on a statement can't be reached after three minutes of discussion, agree to set it aside for discussion at the next meeting. Make brief notes about the grounds for disagreement and what, if any, new information should be brought to everyone's attention. Ask each member to bring additional ideas and thoughts on the topics to the next meeting.
- At your next meeting, revisit the statements which could not be agreed upon earlier. Limit discussion of each item to three minutes, then vote, thumbs up or down, for recommended Action Choices 1 (push upward) or 2 (delete). If agreement is not reached, Choice 3 (selective abandonment) is the default position.

Action Item C: Share the work of each grade-level group with the entire staff

Before the meeting, provide a brief overview of the developmental stages and examples of age-appropriate and age-inappropriate curriculum content for any classroom teachers who did not participate with their grade-level team. At the meeting, discuss and answer questions. Schedule a second meeting time to come to agreement on the project. Work toward consensus; vote only when you have to.

Action Item D: Invite your district curriculum director to get involved

Invite your district curriculum director to get involved in this project because age appropriateness is a districtwide concern. Request that he or she meet with your steering committee and attend a sampling of grade-level work-group meetings as well as the meeting of staff as a whole. Make sure the results of your work are shared with the superintendent and board. Also, request in writing that the district approve your committee's recommendations.

ACTION TASK 2: ANALYZE HOW WELL YOUR STANDARDS ENHANCE PATTERN SEEKING

Action Item E: Prepare to analyze

Once curriculum content is pared down to what is age appropriate, *prepare to analyze* how well your curriculum enhances students' ability to seek patterns (Step One of the learning process). Have the curriculum steering committee do the following:

- Select the subject area you want to begin with; choose only from among those that have already been analyzed for age appropriateness.
- Aim for consensus.

- Create a spreadsheet like the one in Figure 8C to be used by each grade-level committee. List each curriculum standard for each grade level in the first column. (This could be done by a parent volunteer.)
- Train several teachers, preferably one per grade level, to become expert in enhancing pattern seeking.

Analysis of Enhancing Pattern Seeking

Grade Level _____	Factoid–to–Conceptual 1 2 3 4 5	Recommended Action
Curriculum Standard		OK | R | C | D
•		
•		
•		

Legend for the Factoid-to-Conceptual Scale:

1 -- 3 -- 5

Factoid	**Neither a Factoid nor a Concept**	**Conceptual**
Provides no or little pattern to engage the brain	Knowledge of significance, but lacks context and transferability and generalizability; it thus provides limited pattern seeking	**and thus rich in pattern** Generalizable and transferable

Recommended Action:

OK = Okay as is

R = Revise it—rewrite to make it more conceptual

C = Cluster it with a related concept (identify that concept in the right margin)

D = Delete it

Figure 8C

Action Item F: Tasks for each grade-level committee

- Begin with an overview of the brain as pattern seeker and Step One of the learning process (see Appendix A). Answer any questions about the information and the research behind it and then work through the curriculum for that grade level.
- Assign a member of the committee to serve as resident expert on brain research and the application of Step One of Two-Step Learning.
- As a committee, analyze the content of your grade level for its ability to enhance students' ability to seek patterns (Step One of the learning process). How conceptual versus "factoidish" is it? Use a

rating scale, such as the one previously described, to assess each standard (sentence or paragraph) in your curriculum. Complete the spreadsheet. Be sure to use the expertise of your work group's resident expert on pattern seeking.

- Aim for consensus. If agreement on a statement can't be reached after three minutes of discussion, agree to set it aside for discussion at the next meeting. Make brief notes about the grounds for disagreement and what, if any, new information needs to be brought to everyone's attention. Ask each member to bring additional forward-looking ideas and thoughts on the topics to the next meeting.

- At the next meeting, revisit the statements that could not be agreed upon earlier.

- For every standard that ranks three or less on the "factoid-to-conceptual" scale, decide what to recommend: Revise, cluster (identify with what), or delete. For help in "bumping up" a standard that is not conceptual enough to enhance pattern seeking, see *Exceeding Expectations: A User's Guide to Implementing Brain Research in the Classroom*, 4th ed., Chapter 13, especially pages 13.4–7.

- Create a first draft of a pacing guide for curriculum that meets your criteria for both age appropriateness and capacity to enhance pattern seeking. List the standards you expect teachers to address in each grading period (when and what order should be up to the teachers). Approach this task as a means to assess *how realistic the amount* of content is (or isn't). Revisit this list at least annually as you continue to refine your curriculum. Remember to make liberal use of the principle of "selective abandonment."

Action Item G: Share the work of each grade-level group with the entire staff

Before the meeting, for any classroom teachers that did not participate with their grade-level team, provide an overview of the brain as pattern seeker and Double-Link Curriculum, including curriculum examples. At the meeting, discuss and answer questions. Schedule a second meeting time to come to agreement on the project. Work toward consensus; vote only when you have to.

Action Item H: Keep your district curriculum director involved

Keep your district curriculum director involved in this project because enhancing pattern seeking through conceptual curriculum is a districtwide concern. Request that he or she meet with your steering committee and attend a sampling of grade-level work-group meetings as well as the meeting of staff as a whole. Make sure the results of your work are shared with the superintendent and board. Also, request in writing that the district approve your committee's recommendations.

Action Item I: Prepare a cost estimate for later use

Each standard rated three or less needs work. The program improvement potential here is enormous but so is the amount of work because once the curriculum is set, you will likely need to budget for new tools and different assessment instruments and for professional development. Begin improvements here only when your work for Chapters 1 through 7 and 10 is well under way and when Action Task 1 of this chapter has been completed for the targeted subject area (or part of a subject area).

RESOURCES

Because making curriculum conceptual is so very critical to Two-Step Learning, all teachers must have a clear picture of what conceptual curriculum looks like for their grade level. Here are some examples of Link-One curriculum. (See also *Science Continuum of Concepts, K–6* by Karen D. Olsen 2009).

Examples of Link-One Curriculum

Anchor Concepts

The following are examples of concepts[8] powerful enough to anchor and organize curriculum for an entire year. Although they clearly originate from science, they have no borders. Each of these organizing concepts could be used to explore language, grammar, the composition of a paragraph, mathematics, social studies, art, and so on. They are umbrellas for related concepts and their patterns.

> Kindergarten: *Exploration:* We can learn about things around us by carefully observing them, comparing them, and doing something to them.

> First Grade: *Basic Needs:* All living things, including humans, have basic needs that their habitat provides.

> Second Grade: *Form and Function:* Physical characteristics of living things vary greatly and determine what they can do and how they do it to meet their basic needs. Similarly, the physical characteristics of nonliving things vary greatly and determine what changes can occur and how they can be used.

> Third Grade: *Change:* Things are changing around us all the time. Change can occur in a variety of ways and for different reasons. Rate and size of change may require tools to observe and measure change. Change can be helpful, harmful, or neutral.

Fourth Grade: *Interdependence:* Within a habitat, resident plants and animals interact with each other and their environment to meet their basic needs.

Fifth Grade: *Systems:* All structures and systems, living and nonliving, are made up of smaller parts and/or processes.

Sixth Grade: *Constancy and Change:* Both living and nonliving systems have situations in which they change and other situations in which they remain unchanged. Change or constancy in a system can be explained in terms of particular variables. Much change in our world is human made, some intended and some not.

Concepts That Connect

An anchor concept is powerful in its ability to connect to other concepts—some of which are components or parts of the anchor concept itself and others of which are simply related by virtue of their intertwined connection in the real world. In any case, what is important is that concepts are patterns that connect to other concepts/patterns.

Example 1: "A system is a collection of things and processes (and often people) that interact to perform some function." This concept, a component of the organizing concept for fifth grade, invites an exploration of science—ecosystems, mechanical engineering, and so forth. But it is also a powerful lens through which to view civics: "Our democratic government is a collection of things (laws, government agencies, and citizens) and processes (those described in or allowed by laws)." Economics? Yes. Supply and demand are two interacting components of the capitalist system. Art? Of course. The Munsell Color Wheel is a system of analyzing color combinations and intensity of hue. Music? Yes. Any musical score can be looked at as a system involving melody, harmony, rhythm, and so on. Also, algebra. Or a sentence or paragraph. The potential for integration goes on and on.

Example 2: Consider the rich exploration that could come from study through a related concept: "To study a system one must define its boundaries." For example, in science, a watershed can't be studied if its boundaries aren't established.

History/social studies: Our federal constitution and the Bill of Rights set the boundaries of our government. Laws considered outside this boundary are considered unconstitutional and are set aside or repealed. (Without such boundaries, there would be chaos.) This concept could be expressed as, "Our federal constitution and Bill of Rights set the boundaries of our government. Democratic governments are rule-based systems of government rather than power-based forms, such as dictatorships, oligarchies, monarchies, and theocracies."

Boundary lines could also be drawn to include philosophical precursors to our constitution such as the Declaration of Independence, the writings of Thomas Paine, and the constitution of the Iroquois Confederation.

Punctuation draws boundaries around a complete thought (a sentence sets the boundaries for grammar, and a paragraph sets the boundaries for details that explain a thought or position).

In essence, concepts are like computer worms. Once they infect your hard drive, they never stop moving; once they lodge in your brain, your brain keeps extending the patterns, using them to make sense of more and more of the external world.

(Side Note: The most important curricular issue for Link-One curriculum is whether or not your curriculum is conceptual and thus rich in patterns to engage the brain. If your school's curriculum was adopted from your state standards, as most are, your curriculum may be in good shape. Or not. If your state standards are filled with factoids and age-inappropriate content, you will need to do some adapting.)

Sources for Further Study

For further study see the following:

- Appendices A and C.
- *Exceeding Expectations: A User's Guide to Implementing Brain Research in the Classroom*, 4th ed. (2009), especially Chapters 4 (vol. 1) and 12 through 14 and 16 (vol. 3).
- *Science Continuum of Concepts, K–6* (2009).
- *Human Brain and Human Learning*, 3rd ed., by Leslie A. Hart, especially Chapters 7 and 8.

ENDNOTES

1. A typical timeline for revising curriculum is at least two years to revise, adapt, or adopt a new curriculum and three to five years to implement it, depending, of course, on the amount of support and professional development throughout the process. Budget cutting, which would precede the above, would add another year.

2. The brain-based definition of learning, summarized on page 3.7, was first described by Leslie A. Hart in 1975, and then again in 1983 in *Human Brain and Human Learning*, 1st ed. Goldberg, in 2001, reaffirmed Hart's view of learning and provided the science behind the precise shifts in the brain as it learns something new. Ratey (in *Spark: The Revolutionary New Science of Exercise and the Brain.* [New York: Little, Brown and Company, 2008], 42) adds further substantiation: "Patterns of thinking and movement that are automatic get stored in the basal ganglia, cerebellum, and brain stem—primitive areas that

until recently scientists thought related only to movement. Delegating fundamental knowledge and skills to these subconscious areas frees up the rest of the brain to continue adapting, a crucial arrangement." Soldiers in the heat of battle, for example, can't take time to stop to think about how to multiply or add to determine range. The skill must be automatic. And so should it be in the classroom. Every basic skill—that's why we call them "basic" skills—should become automatic, the final phase of Two-Step Learning. The conscious brain needs to be freed up to think about the problems at hand and not be distracted by the mechanics of how to carry out ways to solve them.

However, as Bob Sylwester points out, it's important to also realize that automatic response patterns underlie such culturally negative things as stereotyping, bigotry, and so on. Thus, it's essential that classrooms nurture reflective thinking, guided and independent, during which students reflect on what they're learning and judge the content and weigh the behaviors against their internal compass. Subconscious selection of mental programs need not mean unconscious or insensitive selection.

This is yet one more reason why Link-Two curriculum content should be based in real-life settings where the observation of program selection and implementation of an appropriate behavior provides a rich laboratory for editing, practicing, and wiring into long-term memory programs that will serve students now and throughout life.

3. Susan J. Kovalik and Karen D. Olsen, *Exceeding Expectations: A User's Guide to Implementing Brain Research in the Classroom*, 4th ed. (Federal Way, WA: The Center for Effective Learning, 2009), 13.4.

4. Frank Smith, *Insult to Intelligence: The Bureaucratic Invasion of Our Classrooms* (New York: Arbor House, 1986).

5. This piece of wisdom came from Larry Lowery some years ago when he was head of the Lawrence Hall of Science, UC Berkeley, and science trainer for the Mid-California Science Improvement Program. He has been a tireless proponent of ensuring that the curriculum content we offer children is what they can understand and thus get excited about and love. Lowery was a consultant to the California State Department of Education's science curriculum development committee for several cycles. See his book *Thinking and Learning: Matching Developmental Stages With Curriculum and Instruction.*

6. If this position on age-inappropriate curriculum sounds brash or, even worse, flippant or irresponsible, my apologies. In response, let me share a story: When a science content trainer for the MCSIP program, an outstanding high school science teacher, heard that we were deleting some curriculum topics from each grade level because they were age inappropriate, he was appalled. How dare we! We had no authority to do so! Yet when we asked him if he ever had a student who remembered any of the content from the "To Be Abandoned" list, he admitted the answer was no. Not a single student, even the best and the brightest science students. So please consider: What sense does it make to teach content that students can't understand? If there were a shortage of things to teach students at each developmental level, well then, perhaps . . . take a stretch. However, there is *no* shortage of concepts and content for students at each and every developmental level. We would do well to remember that "to every thing there is a season. . . ."

7. Kovalik and Olsen, *Exceeding Expectations*, Chapter 20, 20.6.

8. Karen D. Olsen, *Science Continuum of Concepts, K–6* (Black Diamond, WA: Books for Educators, 2009).

ACTION SUMMARY CHECKLISTS

Action Task 1: Analyze Your Curriculum for Age Appropriateness

_____ Action Item A: Tasks for the steering committee:
- Select the subject area to begin with.
- Aim for consensus.
- Create a spreadsheet to record your analysis of age appropriateness.
- Train several teachers to become experts in age-appropriate learning.

_____ Action Item B: Tasks for grade-level teams:
- Begin with an overview of developmental stages of the brain.
- Compare each standard to the description of age-appropriate content in Appendix C. For each age-inappropriate standard, recommend what to do with it.
- Aim for consensus.
- At your next meeting, revisit the statements that could not be agreed upon earlier. If agreement is not reached, choice 3 is the default position.

_____ Action Item C: Share the work of each grade-level group with the entire staff.

_____ Action Item D: Invite your district curriculum director to get involved.

Action Task 2: Analyze How Well Your Standards Enhance Pattern Seeking

_____ Action Item E: Once curriculum content is pared down to what is age appropriate, _prepare to analyze_ for pattern enhancement. Have the curriculum steering committee

- Select the subject area to begin with.
- Aim for consensus.
- Create a spreadsheet to record your analysis of age appropriateness.

- Train several teachers to become experts in age-appropriate learning.

_____ Action Item F: Tasks for each grade-level committee:

- Begin with an overview of the brain as pattern seeker and Step One of the learning Process (see Appendix A). Answer any questions about the information and the research behind it and then work through the curriculum for that grade level.
- Assign a member of the committee to serve as resident expert on brain research and the application of Step One of Two-Step Learning and Link-One curriculum.
- As a committee, analyze the curriculum using the scale for conceptual versus factoid. Complete the spreadsheet. Be sure to use the expertise of your work group's resident expert on pattern seeking.
- Aim for consensus.
- For every standard ranking three or less on the "factoid-to-conceptual" scale, decide what to recommend: Revise, cluster (identify with what), or delete.
- Create a first draft of a pacing guide for curriculum that meets your criteria for both age appropriateness and capacity to enhance pattern seeking.

_____ Action Item G: Share the work of each grade-level group with the entire staff.

_____ Action Item H: Keep your district curriculum director involved.

_____ Action Item I: Prepare a cost estimate for later use. Include costs for new tools, different assessment instruments, and professional development.

9

Double-Link Curriculum for Two-Step Learning— Link Two

A s noted in Chapter 8, curriculum is not an area with high potential for budget cutting. It is also an expensive, very time-consuming realm to improve. However, when you're ready, you will find a big return on your investment.

> *$ Cutting Potential—0*
>
> *Cost-Efficiency Ratio—8*

Before you begin working with Link-Two content, make sure that Link-One content is exactly the way you want it—and stated as conceptually as possible—because although "doing" activities usually stir up considerable interest and excitement in students, they are a good investment *only if* they provide specific, targeted practice applying a particular standard in your curriculum.

Again, the best strategic approach is to keep the task of improving curriculum on the back burner until the tasks for Chapters 1 through 7 and 10 are well under way and work on Link-One curriculum is completed and sufficient to support work on Link Two.

LINK-TWO CONTENT

Link-Two curriculum, explored in this chapter, provides the content to help students develop programs for using Link-One content and wiring it into long-term memory. In most schools, Link-Two curriculum is nearly nonexistent. The low sensory input of workbooks and worksheets is woefully inadequate to the task of nudging physiological change in the brain and certainly stops short of wiring the learning into long-term memory (except for paper-and-pencil tasks such as writing). Teachers, then, must scramble to create Link-Two content on their own.

Chain Links as a Metaphor

The metaphor of curriculum as a double-link chain is based in the brain-research-based definition of learning as a two-step process and carries with it what we know about chains:

- The two links parallel the two steps of the Two-Step Learning process—pattern seeking and program building.

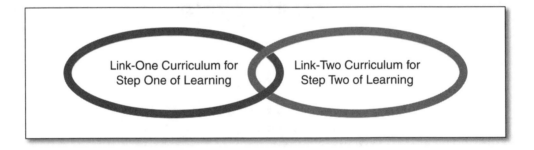

- All links of a chain are designed for the same purpose or load; chains are not composed of links of different sizes or shapes or tensile strengths. In the case of curriculum, the two links are connected to do the same job. In other words, the content of Link Two must be specifically designed to help students apply and wire into long-term memory the content of the specific standard identified in Link One; both links are designed to do the same job (as defined by Link One).
- A chain, however short, is only as strong as its weakest link. If the content of Link One does not enhance students' ability to detect and make meaning, the content of Link Two has no focus and is wasted.
  - o Conversely, however good the content of Link One, if the content of Link Two doesn't provide sufficient practice in applying that particular concept or skill until wired into long-term memory, learning will not occur.

- A chain is an item to be used. The content of Link Two consists of activities for using concepts and skills (Link-One content) in real-world situations—the kinds of situations that students have already had experience with and those they see people around them facing on a daily basis. *Being there* experiences are critically important content for both links. (See definition in the Glossary.)

See the Resources section of this chapter for an example of curriculum that fits this double-link metaphor.

Curriculum Content for Step Two of Learning

Link-Two curriculum must be action based, application oriented, result focused, and directed toward solving problems and producing products. To do so in an authentic way, curriculum must be based in *being there* locations—study trip sites chosen to best teach each chunk of curriculum. This allows students to see the concepts and skills of the standards as they are utilized in real life. And there must be enough Link-Two curriculum for each Link-One concept or skill to give sufficient practice for each student to wire that concept or skill into long-term memory.

As mentioned earlier, few curricula provide Link-Two content for teachers. This is unfortunate because teachers, working in isolation, are unlikely to have the time to develop resources of sufficient quantity and quality to enable students to complete learning at Stage Two.

For more information about developing curriculum for Link-Two curriculum, see *Exceeding Expectations: A User's Guide to Implementing Brain Research in the Classroom*, 4th ed., especially pages 13.9–17, 14.7–16, and 17.1–5 (vol. 3).

ACTION ITEMS

Action Item A: Tasks for the steering committee

Tasks for the steering committee (likely the same committee created for Action Item A, page 1.4) are as follows:

- Select the subject area you want to begin with. *Recommendation:* Select from among the subject areas (or sub areas) that have been revised following the work for Chapter 8.
- Determine whether work completed for Link One in your chosen area, as described in Chapter 8, is sufficient to serve as a base for work on Link-Two content. If not, do not proceed with this subject

at this time. Either select another subject area whose Link-One curriculum is adequate or disband your committee for now.
- Aim for consensus.
- Train several teachers, preferably one per grade level, to become experts in Step-Two Learning and Link-Two curriculum.
- Create an analysis sheet, such as the one in Figure 9A, for each of the grade-level committees to use. List each standard in the first column. (For an example, see Figure 9B. This task could be done by a parent volunteer.)
- Activate the grade-level curriculum committees.

Chart for Analyzing Link-Two Curriculum

Curriculum Standard/ Link-One Curriculum*	Existing Link-Two Curriculum**	Helps students build programs§ and write them into long-term memory 1 2 3 4 5
•		
•		

Legend for the "build programs" scale:

1 ------------------------ 2 ---------------------- 3 --------------------- 4 ------------------------ 5

Not at all	**Minimal**	**Somewhat effective**	**Effective**	**Very effective**
Provides little or no practice using the stated concept or skill	In quality and quantity	Fairly effective but very limited in amount	But limited in amount	Very effective and sufficient quantity

* The statement of the standard has been made as conceptual as possible; skills are stated exactly as students are to remember and use them.

** *List only* those resources/materials that rated "above the line" when you analyzed for sensory input, page 2.5, *AND* that are *precisely selected* to teach students how to apply the particular Link-One curriculum statement as identified. "Somewhat related" should not be included.

§ Apply this scale to all the Link-Two resources and materials used to teach a particular curriculum statement or standard—*taken as a whole*, not item by item.

Figure 9A

Example of Link-Two Curriculum Analysis

Curriculum Standard/ Link-One Curriculum*	Existing Link-Two Curriculum**	Helps students build programs§ and write them into long-term memory 1 2 3 4 5

• Most systems-smaller
  parts
	7 inquiries for Concept Key Pt. 2
	2 homework assignments
	  (page 9.8)
		4

• To study system, boundaries	There are no existing resources that are "above the line"***	1

Legend for the third column—the "build programs" scale:

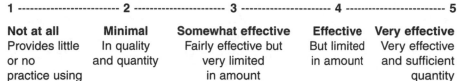

Not at all	**Minimal**	**Somewhat effective**	**Effective**	**Very effective**
Provides little or no practice using the stated concept or skill	In quality and quantity	Fairly effective but very limited in amount	But limited in amount	Very effective and sufficient quantity

*   The statement of the standard has been made as conceptual as possible; skills are stated exactly as students are to remember and use them.

** *List only* those resources/materials that rated "above the line" on sensory input, page 2.5, *AND* are *precisely selected* to teach students how to apply the particular Link-One curriculum statement as identified. "Somewhat related" should not be included.

§   Apply this scale to the Link-Two resources/materials used to teach a particular curriculum statement or standard—*taken as a whole*, not item by item.

*** "Above the line" is a reference to the Sensory Input Analysis chart in Figure 2A on page 2.3.

Figure 9B

Action Item B: Tasks for each grade-level committee

- Involve all classroom teachers in this action item if possible.
- Begin with an overview of Step Two of the learning process (see Appendix B) and Link-Two curriculum. Answer any questions about the information and research.
- As a committee, go back to the results of your Sensory Input Analysis done for page 2.5. Identify all resources and materials that rated "above the line" that also provide students opportunities to apply each Link-One standard listed on the analysis sheet on the previous page.

- Analyze the content of these above-the-line resources to determine its ability to enhance program building and wire concepts and skills into long-term memory (Step Two of the learning process). Complete the analysis (see the example worksheet in Figure 9B). Be sure to use the expertise of your work group's resident expert on Step Two of the learning process.
- Aim for consensus about how existing Link-Two curriculum is actually used at your school, not its potential use. If agreement on an item can't be reached after three minutes of discussion, agree to set it aside for discussion at the next meeting. Make brief notes about the grounds for disagreement and what, if any, new information needs to be brought to everyone's attention. Ask each member to bring additional ideas on the topics to the next meeting.
- At your next meeting, revisit items which could not be agreed upon earlier. Spend no more than three minutes per Link-Two item. If necessary, calculate an average score from the group.
- Note: For every Link-One curriculum standard that has a Link-Two curriculum ranking of 3 or less, mark it for future work. Work only with Link-One curriculum standards that were rated 4 or 5 in Chapter 8.
- Strategize where to place your resources. *Recommendation:* Start small. Quality and mastering the learning curve is far more important than quantity:
  - At each grade level, look for clumps of curriculum whose Link-Two curriculum is rated 4 or better.
  - Build around these islands of strength. Identify other Link-One standards that are glued together by the same strong anchoring concept as these rated 4 or better. Create or revise Link-Two curriculum for these standards that rate a 4 or better.
  - Slate these curriculum chunks for implementation as soon as feasible. Learn from this improvement cycle and apply the lessons to the next round of Link-Two curriculum development. Be patient. Build slowly but well.

- Prepare an estimate of the time and resources needed to complete each step strategized above. Create a timeline for the first three steps.
- Explore what changes in assessment instruments would be appropriate to accompany the changes you're making in Link-Two curriculum.[1] Send your recommendations to the committee working on testing (Chapter 10).

Action Item C: Share the work of each grade-level group with the entire staff

Before the meeting, provide a brief overview of the brain research behind Step Two of the learning process for any classroom teachers who did not participate with their grade-level team. At the meeting, discuss and answer questions. Schedule a second meeting time to come to agreement on the project. Work toward consensus; vote only when you have to.

Action Item D: Invite your district curriculum director to get involved

Invite your district curriculum director to get involved in this project because Link-Two curriculum to help students wire learning into long-term memory is a districtwide concern. Request that he or she meet with your steering committee and attend a sampling of grade-level work-group meetings as well as the meeting of staff as a whole. Make sure the results of your work are shared with the superintendent and board. Also, request in writing that the district approve your committee's recommendations.

RESOURCES

The three resources included are as follows:

- Example of Double-Link Curriculum
- A Word About Assessment
- Sources for Further Study

Examples of Double-Link Curriculum[2]

Conceptual Key Point 1: Most systems are made up of smaller parts that when put together can do things the parts could not do by themselves.

Inquiries[3] for Conceptual Key Point 1:

1. With your Learning Club, investigate the bicycle that is in the classroom. Draw a picture of the bicycle in your Science Journal. Label all the smaller parts that create the bicycle. Explain how they help the bicycle do what it does. Share your list with another Learning Club. Discuss any items where your two Learning Clubs do not agree. Add to your own list any new ideas gained from this sharing. (BK, LM, L) (Note: These initials identify the multiple intelligence(s) called upon by the inquiry. BK = bodily-kinesthetic, LM = logical-mathematical, L = linguistic, S = spatial, M = musical.)

2. Examine the three photos of old-fashioned cycles (unicycle, chainless bicycle, early motorcycle). Choose two to analyze using the Venn circles. Create two sets of Venn circles; compare and contrast the parts of each of the bicycles in the photos with the bicycle in the classroom. Be sure you address the following parts of the system:

source of power, method of translating the power into action, steering, and braking. Work as a Learning Club. Share your findings with the class as a whole. (S, M, L)

3. With a partner, generate questions to ask the guest expert about how bicycles work. Write the questions in your Science Journal. Share your questions with your Learning Club. As a group, decide what two questions you want to ask; decide who will ask the questions. (L, LM)

4. Write a thank-you note to the guest expert. Include at least two things that you were most excited about learning. Include at least two ways you will use this information in the near future. (L)

5. Listen to the song "Bike" by Pink Floyd. Make up movements to accompany the song that demonstrate how the system and subsystems of a bike work. Perform it for the class. (M, LM, BK)

6. With a partner, discuss how our class is part of a larger system. Create a flowchart that shows all of the other parts of this larger system. Post your flowchart on the class bulletin board. Be prepared to explain it to the class. (S, LM, L)

7. Go on a 10-minute walkabout at your school. Identify an item that is part of a system yet small enough to fit in your pocket. In your Science Journal sketch a picture of this object. Write a paragraph telling how it is part of a system. (BK, S, LM, L)

Homework Extension: Repeat the assignment described in Inquiry 1 on the previous page with a parent, sibling, or friend. Add to your list any new ideas you discover about what the parts do and how they help the bicycle do what it does. The next day, share your experience with others in your Learning Club. Compare their discoveries with your own. Add any new ideas you learn to your list. (BK, LM, S, L)

Homework Extension: List in your Science Journal five examples of systems in your home or neighborhood that are good examples of the concept: Most systems are made up of smaller parts that when put together can do things the parts could not do by themselves. Choose two of those systems; label the parts of each. Add two observations about systems that you have made as a result of studying these systems. Share your findings with your Learning Club when you return to school.

Assessment Inquiry: Working on your own, list five examples of systems you see at your school that are good examples of the concept: Most systems are made up of smaller parts that when put together can do things the parts could not do by themselves.

Choose two of those systems to analyze. On two 8.5" × 11" pieces of paper, draw and label the parts of each system; briefly describe what each part does. In one or two sentences, tell what the system does that the parts by themselves cannot do. (Use the back side of the paper if necessary.)

Next, describe two observations about systems that you have made as a result of studying the systems you analyzed. Record these observations on the back side of one of the Venn circles.

A Word About Assessment

As the above assessment inquiry illustrates, assessment for double-link curriculum should be a natural extension of the inquiries themselves—a test of one's ability to use concepts and skills in real-world situations. Especially informative are tasks that require concepts and skills to be applied in varying settings, not rote application to the same setting and/or situation selected for instruction.

For more information about assessment for Two-Step Learning and Double-Link Curriculum, see *Exceeding Expectations: A User's Guide to Implementing Brain Research in the Classroom*, 4th ed., pages 19.1–9 (vol. 3).

Sources for Further Study

For further study, see the following:

- Appendix B.
- *Exceeding Expectations: A User's Guide to Implementing Brain Research in the Classroom*, 4th ed., especially Chapter 5 and pages 13.9–17, 14.7–16, and 17.1–5.
- *Human Brain and Human Learning*, 3rd ed. (2002), Chapters 9 and 10 and pages 258–273. See also the discussion of prosters and biasing, Chapters 4, 10, and 11.

ENDNOTES

1. Inquiries from Link-Two curriculum content can easily be adapted to become criterion reference assessment items. See *Exceeding Expectations: A User's Guide to Implementing Brain Research in the Classroom*, 4th ed. (Federal Way, WA: The Center for Effective Learning, 2009), Chapter 19, especially pages 19.6–9.

2. There are a number of curriculum development models, but few have stood the test of time and academic scrutiny. One such model is the ITI (Integrated Thematic Instruction) model, now referred to as the *Highly Effective Teaching (HET)* model. It is now almost 25 years old and has been used in thousands of schools across the United States, Canada, and abroad (Slovakia, Czech Republic, Italy, Japan, Indonesia, Switzerland, and the Netherlands). In 1999, it was selected by Dr. Charles M. Reigeluth, Professor at Indiana University, as an instructional model that met his stringent criteria for his new paradigm of Instructional Theory (see *Instructional-Design Theories and Models, Vol. 2: A New Paradigm of Instructional Theory* (New Jersey & London: Lawrence Erlbaum Associates, Publishers, 1999). The ITI/*HET* model was also chosen as one of 22 curriculum and instructional models for the Comprehensive School Reform model, a reform effort launched by the U.S. Department of Education in the late 1990s.

3. Adapted from curriculum developed by Deb Meyer for a Kovalik ITI Model Teaching Week.

ACTION SUMMARY CHECKLIST

_____   Action Item A: Create a steering committee.

_____   Action Item B: Tasks for each grade-level committee:
- Assign a member of the committee to serve as resident expert on brain research and the application of Step Two of the learning process and Link-Two curriculum development.
- Begin with an overview of the brain as program developer.
- As a committee, analyze the Link-Two content of your grade level for its ability to enhance program building and wiring concepts and skills into long-term memory. Complete the spreadsheet analysis.
- Aim for consensus. If agreement on an item can't be reached, make brief notes; meet again to discuss.
- For every Link-One curriculum standard that has Link-Two curriculum ranking less than a 4, mark it for future work.
- Strategize where to place your resources.
- Prepare an estimate of the time and resources needed to complete each step strategized above. Create a timeline for the first three steps.
- Explore what changes in testing instruments would be appropriate to accompany the changes you're making in Link-Two curriculum. Send your recommendations to the committee working on testing (Chapter 10).

_____   Action Item C: Share the committees' work with the entire staff. Begin with a brief overview of the brain research behind Step Two of the learning process. Schedule a second meeting time to come to agreement on the strategizing done by the work groups. Work toward consensus.

_____ Action Item D: Invite your district curriculum director to get involved.

- Request that he or she meet with your steering committee.
- Share the results of your work with the superintendent and board.
- Request that the district approve your committee's recommendations.
- Share with the school staff the response of the district to any needed waivers or changes in policy.

10

Testing—Does the Emperor Wear Clothes?

Few disagree that testing has become excessive and overly burdensome. Yet to complain has somehow come to be viewed as un-American or the whimpering of those who don't want to be held accountable or who have something to hide.

$ Cutting Potential—10

Cost-Efficiency Ratio—3

However, in a time of severe budget cutting, even the emperor must be subject to scrutiny. "Does the emperor wear clothes?" is a fair question to ask and one we should feel obligated to ask.

WHAT DO TESTS TEST?

What standardized tests do test has long been debated. Criticism is wide-ranging; charges include cultural bias, testing things that aren't taught in a particular school (and therefore are not a fair test of that school's instructional program), putting unreasonable stress on students, pushing staff into teaching to the test, and more. The list is a long one, including suspicions that No Child Left Behind, with its heavy-handed testing requirements, was designed "as a Trojan horse for the school choice agenda—a way to expose the failure of public education and 'blow it up a bit.'"[1]

My complaint about standardized tests is that they consist primarily of true-false (T-F) and multiple-choice items that do not—and cannot—measure learning as now defined by brain research.

STANDARDIZED TESTS DON'T TEST LEARNING

Although T-F and multiple-choice questions are less expensive to score, they do *not* measure learning as defined by brain research. The following graphic, Figure 10A, shows what conventional kinds of test items really measure when compared to this new definition of learning.

Two-Step Learning[2] Versus Types of Test Items

Step 1 Pattern Seeking[3]		Step 2 Program Building[4]	
Making meaning, understanding (input)		Able to use what is understood (output)	
Detecting patterns	Understanding the patterns	Use with conscious effort and guidance	Use automatically and "wired" into long-term memory
Assessment questions:			
Q. What do you want students to understand?		Q. What do you want them to do with what they understand?	
|———————————————|		|———————————————|	
Test Item Type	T-F items Essay questions Multiple choice	Demonstration with real-world situations	Demonstration over time in different settings

Figure 10A

The inconvenient truth about testing is this:

- T-F items can be answered based on the barest of recognition, that little bell in one's head that says, "That choice sounds like something I've heard before." Understand it? No, not needed. One can ace a test composed of true-false and multiple-choice items without understanding the content. This "sound of familiarity" is quickly dumped from short-term memory.
- Multiple-choice questions can also be correctly answered by a combination of bell ring and cagey test-taking savvy. Understand the content? No, not necessary. Since real-life situations rarely provide us with multiple-choice options, test-taking savvy is of little post-school value.

- As for essay questions, memorization can often carry one through the answer—the so-called "parrot back" exercise. In such instances, understanding the content isn't necessary and "application" is usually quite superficial, a memorized application in a limited sphere. Also, the fact that students do understand the content and can talk and write about it doesn't necessarily indicate that they can use what they understand. And certainly, it cannot determine if what they understand has been wired into long-term memory. For example, I can still remember my shock when my college Western Civilization blue-book exam was returned (the grading process took about three weeks). In my very own handwriting was information I'd never heard of before! The content I had "learned" lasted long enough in short-term memory to get me an "A" on the exam but completely evaporated shortly thereafter. Sound familiar?

A Touch of Reality

Here's a test for the reader. Read the paragraph below and answer the questions:

"Cayard forced America to the left, filling its sails with 'dirty air,' then tacked into a right-hand shift. . . . That proved to be the wrong side. America, flying its carbon fiber-liquid crystal main and headsails, found more pressure on the left. Cayard did not initiate a tacking duel until Il Moro got headed nearly a mile down the leg. . . . Cayard did not initiate a jibbing duel to improve his position heading downwind and instead opted for a more straight-line approach to the finish."[5]

1. America was pushed off course and forced to utilize dead air.

   true   false

2. What kind of sail did America have? _____ (fill in the blank)

3. How far down the leg did Il Moro get before Cayard initiated a tacking duel?

   A. Less than a mile   B. One mile

   C. Slightly more than a mile   D. None of the above

We assume this paragraph has something to do with sailing, and we could answer the above questions. However, does answering these questions about this sailing race really mean you understand what is happening in the race or about racing strategy or, even more important, how to sail a boat? No, but we could pass the typical test.

Having the words—or words that sound like the right words—but having no understanding of them often leads to high good humor as in the following student test responses:[6]

- Water is composed of two gins. Oxygin and hydrogin. Oxygin is pure gin. Hydrogin is gin and water.
- H_2O is hot water; C_2O is cold water.
- We do not raise silk worms in the United States because we get our silk from rayon. He is a larger worm and gives more silk.
- A census taker is a man who goes from house to house increasing the population.

However, for the science teacher of these kids, such statements may not seem so funny. They are products of facile young minds bathed in omnipresent media and its unceasing flow of words. As understanding lags considerably behind, misunderstanding is rampant and application superficial to nonexistent.

More Flaws

My complaint about standardized tests . . . they don't measure learning as now defined by brain research.

Additional failings of standardized tests include subject area tests that test reading skill rather than content and items that are culturally out of date, artificial, and even downright tricky and/or pointless.

Test of Reading Skill, Not of Content Knowledge and Skill

Some years ago, I worked with a school board in a retreat setting. They were having trouble working as a group. Because an item of intense disagreement was testing, I had them "take" the 10th-grade science portion of the popular standardized test of the time. To their horror, they discovered that only one item in the entire science test required prior science knowledge. All the other items were simply a test of reading skill.

They were appalled that such tests wasted taxpayers' money and teacher and student time. Worse, they realized the test results provided no useful information for meaningful decision making and squandered community support.

Eliminate such tests and select a different one. If they are state created or federally driven, request a waiver. And register your concerns.

Culturally Out of Date

Items that are culturally out of date ensure incorrect answers. For example, consider the following:[7]

"What item, *1*, *2*, or *3*, best matches the item on the left?"

1   2   3

The correct answer was supposed to be 2, a saucer. However, in an era in which mugs have replaced cups and saucers, few children are likely to choose the "correct" answer. Why, everyone knows that a person uses a spoon to stir a beverage, such as hot chocolate or coffee. What an obvious answer!

Artificial

Artificial items demean the serious student's search for meaning.

"Maria's father has five daughters:

1. Chacha

2. Cheche

3. Chichi

4. Chocho

5. ??????

What is the name of the fifth daughter?"[8]

Now, I don't know about you, but I don't know a single soul that goes through life expecting to solve life's problems by applying the sequence of the five vowels of the English language: a, e, i, o, u.

Ah! But it's not about the vowel sounds. It's about Maria, whose father has five daughters, she being the fifth.

Why do we waste time and money on such items? The response—"correct" or not—is of no value to the classroom teacher for improving learning for students.

Tricky and/or Pointless

Whether this next item is guilty of being tricky or pointless, you decide.

> "You are competing in a race and overtake the runner in second place. In which position are you now?"[9]

So, are you now first? Nope. You're still second.

If we want students to apply logic, they deserve problems worth solving.

Not Useful

Too many standardized tests are too much, too late. Designed to be a score card—usually for the school or a grade level—they provide a composite average over the year. What they don't do—and what should be considered the most important task of assessment—is *provide feedback that enables a teacher to improve his or her teaching on a day-by-day basis.* An F at the end of the year is too late for both teacher and student. Also, knowing that a student is below grade level in reading (or any other subject) doesn't tell the teacher what is holding the student back or where to start or what approach or materials would be most effective.

To be useful, not coercive, assessment should inform the instructional process on a day-to-day basis. Testing for the sake of testing is a waste of time, resources, and the goodwill of students and teachers.

WHERE AND WHAT TO CUT

"Never be afraid to do something new. Remember, amateurs built the ark; professionals built the Titanic."

—Unknown

Nationwide, we spend billions every year on testing that measures only the ring of familiarity and the fleeting content of short-term memory. Yet I suspect few would say this is what we want for our future voters and workers. Getting a high score on a test based on just a hint of familiarity is the wrong message for students and robs them of the awareness of "knowing when we know and knowing when we don't know" and fosters forming firm opinions out of a few facts. From there, poor judgment is just a step away. This is a rich area for both cutting budget *and* making significant program improvements.

HOMEGROWN ISN'T NECESSARILY BETTER

Just because a test is homegrown doesn't mean it's better. Many districts squander money and time on locally developed tests that are no less onerous than standardized tests demanded by federal and state politicians and no better at providing information that would help teachers improve instruction on a day-to-day basis.

ACTION ITEMS

Action Item A: Create an Assessment Study Committee at your school

The selection of stakeholders for this group will be the most challenging of all the groups because differences in points of view are widest and most passionately held. As the amount of resources—time, money, and ability of the tail to wag the dog—is huge here, it's a most critical area. Set the membership, and schedule its calendar. Remember, short meetings held frequently produce far better results than a few, long meetings. Review Action Items A and B and D through I in Chapter 1. Repeat here the steps of group building and group leadership as needed.

Action Item B: Analyze every item or every test

Analyze every test your school gives schoolwide or by grade levels. Using a sample test, read every item to determine what is really being tested. Complete the following spreadsheet for each test item.

Test Item Analysis Form

	Tests Step ___ of Learning Processes		low high Important to our curriculum	Tests only reading, not content	Item out of date	Item artificial	Item tricky or useless	Helps inform instruct
Item #	One	Two	1 2 3 4 5					

Title of Test (or Subtest) _____

For information to help you determine whether an item tests learning at Step One or Two of the learning process, study Appendices A and B. Please take time to study this information carefully.

As you analyze each test item, ask yourself these questions:

- For Step *One* of the Two-Step Learning process: Does this item only require recognition or test savvy? If so, rate it *1a* as shown on the analysis for Test Item #2 (economics). Or does it require that students *understand* and be able to *use* the content or skill? If so, put *1b* in the column.

- For Step *Two* of Two-Step Learning: Does this item require that students know how to use what they understand in real-world ways? If yes, mark it with a *2c*. If you can determine that the use is practiced enough to believe it has been wired into long-term memory, mark it with a *2d* as shown on the chart.

Items that test only at Step One—*1a* and *1b*—tell you little about what students have or have not learned and what they will carry with them in their long-term memories. Tests consisting solely of *1a* and *1b* items are prime candidates for elimination because they fail to assess long-term memory, learning as defined by brain research, and they do nothing to inform instruction when it's most needed—on a day-by-day basis.

Examples of Test Item Analysis[10]

Test Item 1: Economics

Which of the following is the most likely economic explanation for why a local restaurant that is busy and has many loyal customers could go out of business?

A. The restaurant is spending too little on marketing.

B. The restaurant is paying too little for rent, utilities, and food.

C. The restaurant has more customers than it wants and needs.

D. The restaurant's expenses are higher than its revenues.

Title of Test (or Subtest) Economics #1

Item #	Tests Step ___ of Learning Processes		*low* *high* Important to our curriculum 1 2 3 4 5	Tests only reading, not content	Item out of date	Item arti-ficial	Item tricky or useless	Helps inform instruct
	One	Two						
#1	—	—	1	yes	no	yes	yes	no

Analysis: This item tests reading skill alone; no knowledge of economics is needed. It does not inform instruction. For example,

Commentary:

A. If the restaurant is busy, spending too little on marketing is not relevant as customers keep coming.

B. If the restaurant is busy, spending too little on rent, utilities, and food is not relevant as it isn't chasing away customers.

C. More customers than the restaurant wants and needs? Unlikely. If too many customers were a problem, the restaurant could restrict its hours of operation.

D. So, by elimination, *D* must be the right answer. No prior knowledge about economics was needed (not even the vocabulary word *revenues* is needed).

Items like this don't test what they purport to test. They provide no useful information to decision makers at any level.

Test Item 2: Economics

In the United States, which of the following provides the largest source of tax revenue for the federal government?

A. Corporate income tax

B. Property tax

C. Sales tax

D. Personal income tax

Title of Test (or Subtest) Economics #2

Item #	Tests Step ___ of Learning Processes		low high Important to our curriculum 1 2 3 4 5	Tests only reading, not content	Item out of date	Item artificial	Item tricky or useless	Helps inform instruct
	One	Two						
#2	1a	—	2	no	no	no	no	no

Analysis: This item asks for recall of a fact. It does not ask why the information is important or how this information may be related to high unemployment or underemployment statistics or declining revenues for federal, state, and local governments. Because the test item stops at the first stage of Step One of Learning, the wiring into long-term memory is unknown (and unlikely).

Test Item 3: How the United Nation operates

Imagine that you are the head of the team representing the United States at a model session of the United Nations General Assembly. Student teams from a dozen countries from around the world will also attend. They will discuss the plan you will develop and vote on it.
  Name of Plan: All Children in the World Should Have the Right to Learn to Read and Write.
  Country Writing the Plan: The United States of America
  Please give two reasons why your plan is important for the world.

1.

2.

  Describe one thing the United States can do to support the plan that all children in the world should have the right to learn to read and write.

Title of Test (or Subtest) Civics #3

Item #	Tests Step ___ of Learning Processes		low high Important to our curriculum 1 2 3 4 5	Tests only reading, not content	Item out of date	Item artificial	Item tricky or useless	Helps inform instruct
	One	Two						
#3	—	—	2	no	no	yes	yes	no

Analysis: This item purports to assess fourth graders' understanding of how the United Nations operates. It does nothing of the kind. Understanding how the United Nations operates is superfluous. All this item does is ask students for an opinion about why they think learning to read and write is a right and then to brainstorm one thing that the United States could do to help make that happen.

  This kind of item is an example of smoke and mirrors, providing a facade of sophistication and rigor. It is the kind of test item that misleads decision makers.

Test Item 4: Geography

The information on an accompanying map shows which of the following?

  A. Brazil has a shorter growing season than Argentina has.

  B. New York has a longer growing season than Chicago has.

  C. Canada can grow a greater variety of crops than Florida can.

  D. Colombia can grow a greater variety of crops than Canada can.

Item #	Tests Step ___ of Learning Processes		low high Important to our curriculum 1 2 3 4 5	Tests only reading, not content	Item out of date	Item artificial	Item tricky or useless	Helps inform instruct
	One	Two						
#4	1b	2c	4	no	no	no	yes	no

Title of Test (or Subtest) <u>Geography #4</u>

Analysis: This test item, especially for fourth grade, is very challenging. It requires understanding and ability to apply the concept of length of growing season to crop variety to geography. However, as is often the case, something is built into the test item that ends up making the test item a test of something hidden. For example, the map of the northern hemisphere that accompanies this test item provides color coding to indicate length of growing season; however, in doing so, the lines identifying the location of the nations within the outline of the North, Central, and South American continents are covered up. Thus, the right answer, *D,* could likely be missed, not because a student doesn't know the geography concept but because he or she doesn't know the whereabouts of Colombia (or even Canada) or is mistaken about the relative locations of Brazil and Argentina.

This kind of item sounds rigorous, but the results are useless in assessing student progress in geography or whether or not the teacher taught the state standards.

Action Item C: Rank the tests based on how well they measure the last phase of Two-Step Learning

Rank the tests based on how well they measure the last phase of Two-Step Learning—ability to apply knowledge and skills that are wired into long-term memory.

Discuss your findings as a group. Based on your findings, identify which, if any, of these test are worth keeping.

Action Item D: Do your homework

Get exact costs for each test (actual cost of booklets, answer sheets, scoring and data crunching, courier service, etc.) plus cost of staff time (teaching to the test, test prep, monitoring, data analysis, etc.).

Action Item E: Involve your district office and school board

Invite the appropriate district office staff and members to attend a sampling of staff discussions and presentations to the entire school community.

Action Item F: Present your findings to the entire school community

Continue these discussions through as many meetings—large and small—as it takes until your stakeholders understand your analysis of the tests your school gives, their use, and the implications for budget cutting and reinvestment.

Provide information that will help community members understand the issues at hand. For example, distribute articles presenting a range of opinions about current testing (see the Resources section at the end of this chapter) and the cost of current testing at your school (money and time).

Action Item G: Develop preliminary recommendations to reduce the overall amount of standardized testing

Based on community input from the discussions during Action Item F, develop a set of preliminary recommendations to reduce[11] the overall amount of standardized testing.

For example,

- Eliminate all tests that measure only phases *1a* and *1b* of Two-Step Learning.
- Eliminate all subject area tests that test primarily reading ability, not prior knowledge or skills.
- Test all continuing students every other year or only at specific grade levels (e.g., 2, 5, 8) or test in fewer areas each year or alternate years (e.g., reading one year, math the next).
- During off years, test only incoming students to determine eligibility for special programs.
- To determine promotion out of a special program, base decisions upon assessments that teachers use to monitor student progress and that help them choose the best instructional strategies from day to day.
- Allow parents to request that their child be tested during off years, but at their expense.
- Provide student testing, as needed, for teachers on probation and accountability review.

Action Item H: Ask your school community for support and involve them in the decision making

"We cannot solve problems with the same thinking that created them."

—Einstein

Continue to meet as a school community. Remind participants that there is a lot at stake—for students, for parents, for teachers, and for the current and future budget squeeze. Work toward consensus; implement a process that everyone can respect even if they disagree with the decisions that are made.

Action Item I: Explore all waiver provisions

Explore all waiver provisions available to you—local, state, and federal. For starters, simply go online and search relevant education code provisions regarding waivers. Follow up with calls to the people in charge. Lobby your legislator (state and federal) for any needed changes in rules and regulations as well as laws.

Report your findings to the school community.

Action Item J: Reinvest some of the "saved" money into assessment tools that match the new definition of learning

Some of the funding saved by cutting back on current testing must be reallocated to other kinds of assessment tools that match the new definition of learning. This will require both time and thought. To buy time, consider the following:

- Start now. Assessment tools that assess learning as a two-step process and measure what your school wants taught probably don't exist or exist piecemeal. Take time to find out what's available and what you will need to create to best fit your school's curriculum.
- Be patient. Don't just pounce on the first good idea that comes along. Good assessment is tied to—enmeshed in—curriculum and is part of the instructional process. Make sure that your curriculum is as aligned with Two-Step Learning as you can possibly make it. Until then, hold off selecting or developing new assessment tools.
- To help you with your thinking, do some research. Don't try to make decisions based on the current knowledge base of your staff and parents.
- Understand that assessment for the new definition of learning is best done as an extension of instruction in the classroom; it should provide feedback to the teacher as students practice applying what they understand in real-world situations, not with paper-and-pencil assessments. In a word, *assessment tools should measure the extent to which students have wired the content or skill into long-term memory.*
- To get the most out of your dollars, you should reexamine your curriculum and instructional program. Is your curriculum as conceptual as it could be? Do your instructional practices and Link-Two curriculum carry students through developing a program and wiring it into long-term memory? If not, invest in improving your curriculum and instruction before you invest in improving your assessment tools. Or

more realistically, do both simultaneously as you progress from one subject area (or part of a subject area) to another.

- Remember that the core mission of public education is to educate our citizenry and prepare them to cast informed votes in the voting booth. Thus, aiming our instruction and assessment tools at only the beginning stage of learning is unacceptable.
- Visit schools that have significantly reduced their testing, are implementing curriculum and instruction aimed at Two-Step Learning, and have adopted or developed useful assessment tools.

For more information about creating classroom measures capable of assessing Two-Step Learning, see *Exceeding Expectations: A User's Guide to Implementing Brain Research in the Classroom*, 4th ed., Chapter 19 (vol. 3).

In summary, testing is an area of program and budget that should be cut, *but* it's essential that you reinvest some of the saved funds to create tools and improve curriculum and instruction. In the contentious arena of budget cutting, this is as good as it gets—cutting and improving program at the same time.

RESOURCES

More About Step One of Learning— Pattern Seeking, Making Meaning

For a quick tutorial on the first part of learning, see Appendix A.
For further study, see the following:

- *Human Brain and Human Learning,* 3rd ed. (2002) by Leslie A. Hart, especially Chapters 4, 7, and 8.
- *Brain Rules: 12 Principles for Surviving and Thriving at Work, Home, and School* (2008) by John Medina, especially pages 82–84.
- *On Intelligence: How a New Understanding of the Brain Will Lead to the Creation of Truly Intelligent Machines* (2004) by Jeff Hawkins with Sandra Blakeslee.

More About Step Two of Learning— Developing Useful Programs

For a quick tutorial on developing programs and wiring into long-term memory, see Appendix B.
For further study, see the following:

- *Human Brain and Human Learning,* 3rd ed. (2002) by Leslie A. Hart, especially Chapters 9 and 10.
- *Exceeding Expectations: A User's Guide to Implementing Brain Research in the Classroom,* 4th ed. (2009), especially Chapter 5 (vol. 1).

- *Closing the Achievement Gap: Using the Environment as an Integrating Context for Learning* (1998), Executive Summary by Gerald A. Lieberman and Linda L. Hoody.

Additional Information

"Assessment for Understanding: Taking a Deeper Look" by Roberta Furger, www.edutopia.org/assessment-for-understanding-taking-deeper-look performance assessment. Includes a video of the same name. (Edutopia is a project of The George Lucas Educational Foundation.)

"No Dog Left Behind" by Marion Brady, *Education Week* (January 28, 2009).

"Revolt by Scarsdale Parents," *New York Times* (April 13, 2001).

"Test Today, Privatize Tomorrow: Using Accountability to 'Reform' Public Schools to Death" by Alfie Kohn, *Phi Delta Kappan* (April 2004).

ENDNOTES

1. See "Test Today, Privatize Tomorrow: Using Accountability to "Reform" Public Schools to Death," *Phi Delta Kappan* (April 2004) by Alfie Kohn. Kohn offers an insightful, and scathing, portrayal of the testing quagmire. As he points out, the annual 10% gain requirement of No Child Left Behind (NCLB) is a mathematical impossibility for already high achieving schools. As a result, those schools show up on the "failing schools" list, further shaking the public's confidence in their schools. The Trojan horse quote is from Susan Neuman, an assistant secretary of education during the roll-out of NCLB.

2. For a discussion of the brain research behind the Two-Step Learning Process, see summary on page 2.3 and Appendices A and B. Note the two phases within the two steps. These are useful to analyze test items with greater precision as well as to develop curriculum, choose instructional strategies, and plan lessons.

The idea that we learn by detecting and understanding patterns and then developing programs for using what we understand was first proposed by Leslie A. Hart almost 30 years ago (see *Human Brain and Human Learning*, 3rd ed. [Black Diamond, WA: Books for Educators, 2002], 117). It since has become the standard description of how the brain learns. For examples, see *Brain Rules: 12 Principles for Surviving and Thriving at Work, Home, and School* by John Medina, especially Rule 4: Attention, 82–84, and Rule 5: Short-Term Memory, 115; *Spark: The Revolutionary New Science of Exercise and the Brain* by John Ratey, 42; and *The Executive Brain: Frontal Lobes and the Civilized Mind* by Elkhonon Goldberg (Oxford: Oxford University Press, 2001), 70. Goldberg provides brain images depicting shifts in brain activity that parallel the Two-Step Learning process. These are useful images for teachers as they lesson plan.

3. See Hart's definition of a pattern, *Human Brain and Human Learning*, 349.

4. See Hart's definition of a program, *Human Brain and Human Learning*, 350.

5. *USA Today* (May 13, 1992), 9.

6. See Kennedy's *Kids Say the Darndest Things!*

7. This test item dates back to the early 1960s. Source unknown. Graphics are by Nita Delk.

8. See Probell's *Brain Teasers.*

9. See Probell's *Brain Teasers.*

10. These four test items are adapted from retired test items on the National Assessment of Educational Progress (NAEP) Web site.

11. No doubt this seems a preposterous idea. After all, standardized testing is currently required by all levels—federal, state, and, more than likely, district. However, the feds and most states allow waivers. Do your homework and present your case.

ACTION SUMMARY CHECKLIST

_____ Action Item A: Create an Assessment Study Committee.

_____ Action Item B: Analyze every test your school gives schoolwide or by grade levels.

_____ Action Item C: Rank the tests based on how well they measure long-term memory, the last phase of Two-Step Learning.

_____ Action Item D: Do your homework.

_____ Action Item E: Involve your district office and school board.

_____ Action Item F: Present your findings to the entire school community.

_____ Action Item G: Develop preliminary recommendations to reduce the overall amount of standardized testing.

_____ Action Item H: Ask your school community for support and involve them in the decision making.

_____ Action Item I: Explore all waiver provisions.

_____ Action Item J: Reinvest some of the "saved" money into assessment tools that match the new definition of learning.

Appendix A—Pattern Seeking

O ver 80 years ago, Aldous Huxley wrote, "What emerges most strikingly from recent scientific developments is that perception is not a passive reception of material from the outside world; it is an active process of selection and imposing of patterns."[1]

The findings Huxley referred to were well known in fields more scientifically oriented than education at the time and that are thoroughly established now. Today's brain researchers accept this as a given. We do not have to look far for confirmation—our own

> "Step One of Learning—the extraction, from confusion, of meaningful patterns."
>
> —Leslie A. Hart

daily experience tells us most convincingly that the brain has this ability and has it to an astounding degree. But first, an overview.

LEARNING IS A TWO-STEP PROCESS

Without question, the most powerful insights from brain research lead us to a new definition of learning,[2] a definition that focuses on increasing students' ability to act upon the world in useful and appropriate ways.

Excerpts from *Human Brain and Human Learning,* 3rd ed., by Leslie A. Hart, pages 108–116 & 118, are used here by written permission of the publisher.

Two-Step Learning Process

Step One—Input stage: Pattern seeking and making meaning

First, the brain must detect and identify a pattern;

Second, the brain must make meaning of the pattern, including its relationship to other patterns;

and

Step Two—Output stage: Building programs to use what we understand

The brain must develop programs to use what it understands:

- Begins with conscious effort (often with guidance)
- With practice, becomes almost automatic and wired into long-term memory

---

There is an assessment equivalent of these two steps:[3]

- What do you want students to understand?
- What do you want students to do with what they understand?

THE FIRST FUNDAMENTAL OF LEARNING = STEP ONE OF THE LEARNING PROCESS— PATTERN SEEKING AND MAKING MEANING

According to Leslie A. Hart, the first to describe learning as a two-step process, "The brain detects, constructs, and elaborates patterns as a basic, built-in, natural function. It does not have to be taught or motivated to do so any more than the heart needs to be instructed or coaxed to pump blood."[4]

Hart defines a pattern as

An entity, such as an object, action, procedure, situation, relationship, or system, which may be recognized by substantial consistency in the clues it presents to a brain, which is a pattern-detecting apparatus. The more powerful a brain, the more complex, finer, and subtle patterns it can detect. Except for certain species' wisdom patterns, each human must learn to recognize the patterns of all matters dealt with, storing the learning in the brain. Pattern recognition tells what is being dealt with, permitting selection of the most appropriate program in brain storage to deal with it. The brain tolerates much variation in patterns (we recognize the letter *a* in many shapes, sizes, colors, etc.) because it operates on the basis of probability, not on digital or logic principles. Recognition of patterns accounts largely for what is called insight, and facilitates transfer of learning to new situations or needs, which may be called creativity.[5]

As the brain attempts to make sense out of the chaos which surrounds each of us, it constantly searches for patterns that can impose meaning on the input received. Its "aha" arises from detection of a recognizable (from the learner's perspective) pattern or patterns. This pattern detection propensity is seen in the operation of each of the senses. The ear registers every sound wave within its perceivable frequency, but it attends only to those that provide a meaningful pattern. Sounds of traffic or workshop chatter are ignored, and only the presenter's voice is tuned in or noted as a pattern to attend to. Similarly, the eye recognizes a chair, be it a three-legged milking stool, a church pew, or the more common no-frills chair at the kitchen table; it does so by looking for the pattern or collection of attributes necessary for something to be a chair when one wants to sit down. Other examples include seeing just pointed ears on a wedge-shaped face and a tail and concluding the animal is a cat or recognizing the letter *T* written by many different people or in different computer fonts, for example

$$t \quad \mathcal{T} \quad t \quad \mathrm{T} \quad \mathcal{T} \quad \mathit{T} \quad t \quad \mathbf{T}$$

From the time we are born until we die, the brain takes in these patterns as they present themselves, sorting and categorizing in an attempt to make sense out of our complex world. Learning takes place when the brain—using past experiences and current context—sorts out patterns to make sense out of new input.

In real-life settings, information comes at the learner in a way that can best be described as rich, random, and even chaotic.[6] Throughout the millennia, the brain has perfected learning within such an environment. Hart summarizes this first step of learning as "the extraction, from confusion, of meaningful patterns."[7]

Examples of the First Fundamental of Learning From Personal Experience

Imagine that you are attending a sporting event. People by the thousands stream by as you find your seats. The merest glance tells you they are all strangers. But now, you see two figures that immediately seem familiar, and in a moment you have identified them as former neighbors, Francine and Peter. Somehow, your brain has picked them out of this vast crowd; somehow, it has separated them from all the other people you know so that you can identify them and greet them warmly by name. There is no question that our human brain can do this—usually effortlessly. (If we look at what we all can do, we begin to glimpse the enormous powers of the brain.)

The feat is even more impressive because you haven't seen these friends for three years and didn't expect to run into them here. Both are wearing clothes you have never seen them in. Francine has a new hairstyle; Peter wears sunglasses that partly hide his features. Yet you recognized them as familiar while they were still 50 feet away.

Clearly, the recognition does not stem from any logical process. You did not check Francine's height in inches or Peter's weight in kilos. You put no measure to their middle finger bones, Bertillon fashion, nor did you use a color-comparison guide to determine the shade of skin and hair. While Peter has a distinctive walking movement and Francine an animated manner, trying to measure or describe these exactly would be an impossible task. Let us grasp firmly the clear fact that your brain does not work that way but that it did quickly and accurately accomplish recognition and identification by some other means.

Nor was this an isolated, unusual phenomenon. If I were to display a teakettle, a paint brush, a handsaw, a necklace, a bunch of carrots, a pencil sharpener, a violin, a telephone, a sweater, a microscope, a toothbrush, a slice of Swiss cheese . . . you would recognize and name each in the same effortless way. You were plainly not born knowing these objects, so this recognition has been learned at some time between birth and the present.

We are so used to looking at something and immediately knowing what it is that we come to think of the process as automatic. Comparisons of eye and camera may also mislead us. A camera can't recognize anything; our brain can, using not only vision but also hearing, smell, touch, and other aspects of our senses.

When we are exposed to something quite unfamiliar, we simply do not see it in any meaningful way. To look inside some complex machine, for example, we may see only a confusion of forms. In a museum, observing some fossilized remains of various ancient animals, we may see only vague shapes in contrast to what the curator sees. I often dramatize this in workshops by showing a newspaper in Arabic or Chinese. The participants see only squiggles that a moment later they are hopelessly unable to reproduce—although a person knowing the language would see headlines and news, information at a glance.

If we place a teakettle before a month-old infant, the baby will regard it with momentary interest but plainly have no notion of what it is. As adults, we can see a vessel, a handle, and a spout; the baby can see none of this arrangement, only edges, shapes, and surfaces.

Even if the teakettle were made of unfamiliar materials or shaped like an elephant, we would recognize it as a teakettle. Any familiar item, from a paint brush to a necklace, would be identifiable. Moderate differences do not bother us a bit.

Examples From Classroom Life

Consider, for instance, the 20 different forms of the letter *a* that appear below. Despite the range of shapes they cover, we have no difficulty seeing any one as *a*.

We could, of course, carry this recognition much further, to letters of many larger sizes, in different colors, formed of lights or dots, put into three-dimensional materials, tilted, laid on the floor, or seen on the side of a moving vehicle. Even holding just to typefaces available for printing, there are literally thousands of alphabets; handwritten, drawn, or printed forms add thousands more. There is no letter *a*, only a pattern we conventionally call *a*.

In the same sense, teakettle, paintbrush, carrots, violin, and the rest are patterns. Our knowledge of the pattern is what enables us to say what object is what. But we are by no means limited to hard, visual patterns. We can detect and learn patterns far more subtle or complex. In time, adults normally become quite familiar with such patterns as cat, city park, affection, boss, fraction, racial bigotry, jealousy, or adventurousness.

Just how the brain detects and recognizes patterns cannot be easily or quickly explained. Yet it is an astoundingly powerful, subtle, living computer with billions of neurons at its command. We do know in a general way that the brain detects characteristics or features and also relationships among these features.

The lower-case letter *a*, for example, may consist of a hook facing left, which may take a variety of forms,

connected to a more or less round enclosure form.

a a a a a a a

The relationship between these shapes has a key role. If the hook were 20 centimeters tall and the enclosure only a millimeter high, one might have much difficulty seeing it as an *a*. On the other hand, there is a different pattern for small *a* that lacks the hook altogether that we can readily learn to accept

a a a a a a a

as an alternate. It is illogical to have two forms, but as we have seen, logic is the least of the human brain's concerns.

KEY FACTORS IN PATTERN SEEKING

When looking at the brain as a seeker of patterns, consider five key factors: Use of clues and cues, use of multiple sensory input and prior experience, sensitivity to negative clues, categorizing down through patterns within patterns, and using probability.

Use of Clues and Cues

Our brain's ability to detect and identify patterns is impressive for its flexibility. We can be certain about our identification of something without needing to perceive most or even many of its features and relationships. With experience, in fact, we normally become extremely expert in using *clues* (sometimes the term *cues* is used in the same sense) to make very rapid judgments. We would not be able to read at all if we had to study all the features of letters. The capable reader goes much further and uses clues for whole words and even phrases.

Use of Multiple Sensory Input and Prior Experience

In practice, our pattern-detecting ability depends on clues from vision, hearing, touch, or other senses, on behavior and relationships, and/or on the situation. In short, *the ability to detect and recognize patterns depends heavily on our experience, on what we bring to the act of pattern detection and recognition.* The more that experience tells us what we are likely to be looking at, or dealing with, the less detailed, feature-type information we need to jump to a probably correct conclusion.

Sensitivity to Negative Clues

One reason we can rely on little information is the sensitivity of the brain to *negative* clues. When clues do not fit together rapidly within a pattern, or when one or more are jarringly strange or contradictory, our pattern-detecting apparatus quickly senses something wrong. Suppose that I am going to the house of people I have visited a couple of times before, on a dark suburban street where house numbers are hard to find. As I walk toward what seems to be the house, I come to a flagstone walk. It "doesn't feel right," prompting me to retreat and try the house next door. Or perhaps another day I identify an all-black bird as a Brewer's blackbird. When I see a flash of color on the wing, I must revise my identification to "red-winged blackbird."

Patterns Within Patterns: Categorizing Down

In the example of recognizing friends Francine and Peter, only a yes-no kind of decision was involved—they were or were not those individuals. But more common is the detection and recognition of patterns *within* patterns, which leads to finer and finer discriminations, a process called *categorizing down,* a most important aspect of learning. For example, we can detect the pattern "animal," then categorize it down to "dog," and then to "Afghan hound." Or observing a number of people at a gathering, we may categorize further by noting that the people are festively dressed, a "party," and then on seeing a cake with candles, conclude it's a "birthday party."

But we must note that a person from a country where birthday cakes are not a custom would not be prepared to interpret that clue the way we so easily do. Again, what the observer brings to the recognition act—in terms of prior relevant experience and previously acquired knowledge—plays a critical part. (It is startling to observe that in conventional teaching, this absolutely fundamental principle is largely ignored.)

In small children, the process of enlarging pattern detection and extending and refining categorizing-down chains is often clearly observable. A girl just starting to talk may say, "Daddy!" while pointing to any man who comes into sight—we gather she is using *daddy* in the sense of *man*. A little later, guided by such feedback as "No, that is not Daddy—Daddy is at his office," the child may point to any man who comes into the home, whether young cousin or elderly grandfather, as *daddy*. With further feedback, categories gradually get straightened out, and *daddy* is used to mean only one person. It may take much longer for the child to become clear on the fact that her friend also has a daddy (and some years to grasp the relationship). It may take still more time to be able to categorize surely from people to males, to relatives and friends, neighbors, policeman, mailman, Mr. Jackson (who lives next door), as well as boys, girls, and many other subtle relationships.

It seems apparent that the brain must have some kind of organizational process that enables humans to rapidly categorize down patterns as they are detected, so that they can be identified quickly.

Matching

The principle of *matching* is well understood. In simplest terms, one receives an input from outside the brain—for example, visual input that comes from a door. Inside the brain, stored, is a pattern, *door*. If the current input and the stored pattern pretty well match, recognition occurs. Looking in the night sky, one may see any one of several patterns that match up with stored patterns for *moon*. Hearing some sound waves that compose a certain pattern, we recognize it as the word *scarecrow*, since it fairly well fits our stored pattern for scarecrow. The matches do not have to be precise— another principle, *probability*, applies. This permits us to recognize "scarecrow" whether spoken by a child in a thin, high voice or by a man or woman in other pitches and despite various pronunciations. *The brain searches for a probable match.* (If this were not so, we would all have a terrible time trying to read English with its frequently weird spellings!)

Parallel Processing

But to operate effectively, the brain cannot afford to search sequentially through tens of thousands of stored patterns to find the match. It seems likely that patterns are grouped in categories within hierarchies or layers, much as mail is addressed (reading from the bottom up and right to left):

The country (USA)

The state (Connecticut)

The city or town (Bethel)

The street (Maple Avenue)

The house number (628)

The person in that house (Mr. or Mrs.)

This method, we know, quite efficiently makes a match between the letter and one out of more than 250 million inhabitants. If the address (the input) is a little wrong, the letter may still be delivered, but if the error is large, no match can be made, no delivery can occur.

Experimental studies suggest that the brain does not usually need as many as six steps to categorize down. (That investigation is beyond the scope of this book.) Nor is the brain limited to one linear chain of categorizing down (such as that illustrated above in addressing a letter). It can employ many such chains simultaneously, as we have noted. This "parallel processing" enormously speeds recognition. It's like having l,000 clerks sorting the mail rather than just one.

Using Probability . . . Jumping to Conclusions

A variety of studies indicate that the brain naturally works on a *probabilistic* basis. The brain skillfully jumps to conclusions! It isn't an adding machine that must reach a correct total. For example, seeing a creature that has four legs, a tail, fur, and barks at a friend's home, we jump to the conclusion that the pattern *dog* applies. Why not *cat?* Because we pick up negative clues: Cats don't bark and ordinarily don't come aggressively to the door when a stranger enters. Why isn't it a monkey? Because the relationship of limbs is different. The situation also gives clues; we expect to find a dog in a home. If we visited a zoo, however, and found this same animal exhibited in a cage, we would assume it was not a dog but some similar creature. Our experience tells us that dogs are not displayed this way.

THE BRAIN—A MASTER AT EXTRACTING MEANING FROM CONFUSION

This is the process of learning that Frank Smith and others aptly call "making sense of the world."[8] The ability that even infants have to gradually sort out an extremely complex, changing world is nothing short of astounding. And it's natural. But even more surprising still is that we learn *from input presented in a completely random, fortuitous fashion*—unplanned, accidental, unordered, uncontrolled, the polar opposite of didactic classroom teaching.

Consider, for example, the sorting-out problem a child has to grasp for such patterns as *dessert, pie,* and *cake.* Since a great variety of dishes may constitute dessert, the child must extract the idea that meals have a sequence (program) and dessert is the last course. He or she must also learn that *dessert* does *not* mean a particular dish, or even a tight group or class of dishes. *Pie* presents few problems to an adult with years of experience to draw on, but to a toddler, an open pumpkin pie, a crusted blueberry pie, and a lemon pie heaped with meringue topping present little in common. Or does pie mean *round,* the most obvious feature? Unfortunately, many desserts are round, particularly cakes—which vary from pie-like cheesecake, to coffee cake, to layered birthday cake elaborately iced and decorated.

While adults and older siblings may provide gentle, casual, and almost incidental corrective feedback when the child calls a pie a cake or doesn't regard a fruit dish as dessert and cries in frustration, it would be most unusual for anything resembling teaching or instruction to deal with dessert, pie, and cake as subjects. Yet in a few years, from this confused, random exposure and experience, the child has extracted the patterns, gradually coming to see which features and relationships have significance in which settings, and which can be ignored. Frequently, however, the child extracts a pattern that sooner or later has to be revised in the light of new information. For example, everything falls if let go—until someone presents a gas-filled balloon. Children often find the need to revise something disturbing. The world keeps proving more complicated with more exceptions than they had previously thought. Adults have a similar problem; in time, they may become less flexible, cling to old ideas, refuse to revise, and even try to avoid the input that forces the contradiction. "Nonsense... that's crazy... I won't listen... don't bother me!"

Even more amazing is the obvious ability of preschool children to extract rules about language from the quite random speech they hear about them and engage in. We hear such expressions as *sheeps* and *deers,* plurals plainly not picked up from adults or older children. The added *s* makes unmistakably clear that the small child has extracted a general rule for plurals—end with the *s* sound—and is applying it even to what will later be learned as special exceptions. In the same way, most youngsters will use such constructions as "Tommy hitted me," or "I falled down," showing that they have extracted the pattern of past tense and the use of the *ed* sound, again even where there are common exceptions. Yet it would be absurd to expect a three- or four-year-old to explain *plural* or *past tense.*

These familiar experiences and others like them are so prevalent that we cannot reasonably doubt that all of us, at whatever age, *do extract patterns from the quite random, confused mass of input we are exposed to in the course of normal living.* Nor can it be easily denied that the great bulk of practical knowledge we have and use to get along in the world is acquired in this way.

A Word About Rote Memory. The great bulk of general learning occurs through extracting meaningful patterns from confusion. The only other important method is via rote memory. But while "pure" rote learning—straight memorization—appears to suffice, as in the case of learning the alphabet in sequence, even rote learning is greatly helped by detecting the patterns involved where patterns clearly exist, as in the multiplication tables. Or consider the marching band, very much a rote activity. If the patterns in the music and in the maneuvers are understood, learning can be far faster and more certain.

In Summary

In embracing a new definition of learning, it is important that we recognize a new view of the brain:

- The brain is by nature a magnificent pattern-detecting apparatus, even in the early years.
- Pattern detection and identification involve both features and relationships, processes that are greatly speeded up by the use of clues and a categorizing down procedure (i.e., round ears or barks... not a house cat).

- Negative clues play an essential role.
- The brain uses clues in a probabilistic fashion, not by digital "adding up" of clues.
- Pattern recognition depends heavily on the experience one *brings* to a situation.
- Children must often revise the patterns they have extracted to accommodate new experience.

More About Step One of Learning—Pattern Seeking and Making Meaning

For further study, see the following:

- *Human Brain and Human Learning,* 3rd ed. (2002) by Leslie A. Hart, especially Chapters 4, 7, and 8.
- *Brain Rules: 12 Principles for Surviving and Thriving at Work, Home, and School* (2008) by John Medina, especially pages 82–84.
- *On Intelligence: How a New Understanding of the Brain Will Lead to the Creation of Truly Intelligent Machines* (2004) by Jeff Hawkins with Sandra Blakeslee.

ENDNOTES

1. See *The Human Situation* (Lectures at Santa Barbara, 1959), Pierro Ferrucci, ed. (New York: Harper & Row), 173. Also compare George A. Kelley's view: "Man looks at his world through transparent patterns or templates which he creates and then attempts to fit over the realities of which the world is composed." See *A Theory of Personality* (New York: W.W. Norton, 1963), 17.

2. Leslie A. Hart, *Human Brain and Human Learning,* 3rd ed. (Black Diamond, WA: Books for Educators, 2002), 117.

3. These two assessment questions parallel the Two-Step Learning Process. See *Exceeding Expectations: A User's Guide to Implementing Brain Research in the Classroom,* 4th ed. (Federal Way, WA: The Center for Effective Learning, 2009), Chapter 19.

4. Hart, *Human Brain and Human Learning,* 107–108.

5. Hart, 151.

6. Hart, 129–132.

7. Hart, 117.

8. Like Leslie A. Hart, Frank Smith has a way of cutting to the chase. See *Insult to Intelligence: The Bureaucratic Invasion of Our Classrooms* (New York: Arbor House Publishing Company, 1986); Smith's perspective is as relevant today as it was 20 years ago. Also see *The Book of Learning and Forgetting* (New York: Teachers College Press, 1998) and *Reading Without Nonsense* (4th ed., 2005).

Appendix B—
Developing Programs

Extraction of patterns—identifying and making meaning of them—constitutes the first step of the Two-Step Learning process (see Appendix A). But we do not live by sitting in an armchair and detecting patterns. We live by doing, by action. Thus, the second step in learning is the development of mental programs to use what we know—the patterns we have come to understand, be they a concept or a skill. Step Two of the Two-Step Learning process is defined by Leslie A. Hart as "the acquisition of useful programs."[1]

THE SECOND FUNDAMENTAL OF LEARNING = STEP TWO OF THE LEARNING PROCESS— DEVELOPING PROGRAMS TO USE WHAT IS UNDERSTOOD AND WIRING IT INTO LONG-TERM MEMORY

Hart defines a program as

> a sequence of steps or actions, intended to achieve some GOAL, which once built is stored in the brain and "run off" repeatedly whenever the need to achieve the same goal is perceived by the person. A program may be short, for example giving a nod to indicate "yes," or long, as in playing a

> *"Step Two of Learning—the acquisition of useful programs."*
>
> —Leslie A. Hart

Excerpts from *Human Brain and Human Learning,* 3rd ed., by Leslie A. Hart, pages 140–141, 151–153, & 350 are used here with written permission of the publisher.

piece on the piano, which requires thousands of steps. A long program usually involves a series of shorter subprograms, and many parallel variations that permit choice to meet conditions of use. Many such programs are needed, for instance to open different kinds of doors by pushing, pulling, turning, thumbing a button or lever, and so on. Language requires many thousands of programs, to utter each word, to type it, write it in longhand, print it, and so forth. Frequently used programs acquire an "automatic" quality: they can be used, once selected, without thinking, as when one puts on a shirt. Typically, a program is *consciously* selected, then run off at a subconscious level. In general, humans operate by selecting and implementing programs one after another throughout waking hours.[2]

The basic cycle in using programs is as follows:[3]

1. *Evaluate* the situation or need (detect and identify the pattern or patterns). For example, we want to know if we have sufficient money for an item, with sales tax.

2. In response to the incoming patterns, *select* the most appropriate program from those stored. In this example, we need two programs—multiplication and addition.

3. *Implement* the program. So we multiply the sales tax rate times the cost of our item and add it to the cost. (Multiplying and adding are "automatic" skills. We don't have to think about *how* to perform them, only when and for what purpose.)

In other words, to carry on activities, one must constantly select a program from among those stored in the brain and put it to use.

For example, from the moment we wake in the morning until laying our head on our pillow at night, our life is an unrelenting swirl of program cycles, one after the other. Showering (as soon as we grab that bar of soap, it knows just what to do), dressing (the left leg always goes first), driving (who even thinks about putting in and turning the key; in fact, how many times have we driven somewhere and arrived with absolutely no recollection of the trip?). Well-wired programs can be performed subconsciously, almost automatically, while the brain is busy thinking about what we need to accomplish next.

Virtually every basic skill taught in school needs to become a program that can be selected and run off automatically—reading, punctuating a sentence, multiplying, dividing, and so on. They must all be wired into long-term memory as a program that can be selected and operated with no or little conscious thought so that the brain can focus on the bigger picture—comprehending what it is reading or the significance of the answer arrived at by multiplying and dividing. *The important point is that one cannot pull up and use a program* (such as computing a long division problem) *if the program for doing so is not there.*

And not just the basic skills. All skills and all concepts must become part of a useful program (useful from the learner's perspective) and wired into long-term memory or be dumped from short-term memory as irrelevant (often because they were never understood in the first place).

If you're thinking that teaching to this level of competency takes time, you're right. But if we eliminate the long-trumpeted practice of spiral curriculum in favor of teaching a concept or skill development through the Two-Step Learning process the first time, succeeding rounds of lessons on the same thing year after year won't be needed.

The brain is astoundingly nimble and powerful when it is allowed to learn in real-world settings. Time for *being there* experiences needs to replace seat work time. (Refer to the discussion of sensory input in Chapter 2.)

The Mystery of Behavior

For thousands of years, back to the dim origins of humans, behavior has seemed largely a mystery. What people did seemed utterly haphazard, unpredictable, and unexplainable.

Teachers have long struggled with the behavior of their charges, often to the degree that class management threatens to push instruction into a secondary function. Even corporate personnel specialists confess to being frequently surprised and baffled by the behavior of workers, for all the "motivation" that pay and prospects of advancement would seem to offer. More than half of marriages in the United States go astray; the inability of spouses to understand each other, even after years of intimacy, stands out. At any gathering of parents, the difficulties of comprehending the strange worlds children inhabit take a prominent place in the discussions.

However, in the last four decades and more, researchers studying the brain and several other disciplines have made progress on many fronts. When their findings are brought together and unified, our understanding of human behavior can take a great leap. This opens the door to revolutionary advances in education and gives us the chance to catch up, at least somewhat, with the discoveries resulting from the dazzling and often upsetting advances in technology.

THE BASIS OF BEHAVIOR: PROGRAMS

The key to understanding human behavior is the realization that we act very largely by programs. The word *programs* need not alarm us with visions of robots. It means simply a fixed sequence for accomplishing some intended objective. In other words, we act to carry out some purpose, some personal, individual, and usually self-selected purpose—the exact opposite of robot behavior.

Suppose, for example, that I wish to telephone my dentist. I pick up the phone, push the buttons in a certain order, and put the receiver to my ear to wait for the call to go through. I have executed a program for making a phone call. Should I call him again tomorrow, I will go through just about the same procedure.

Should I wish to phone a local store, I may have to use an additional program to find the number. I get the phone book, look up the listing (or more likely, use the Internet), then dial—a variation of the program I used to call my dentist.

If now I want to visit the store, I must implement a longer program. I go to my car, take out my keys, find the right one, unlock the door, open it, get in, put the key in the ignition switch, fasten the seat belt, turn the switch and start the engine, release the parking brake, put the car in gear, press the accelerator pedal—just to start on my trip. To get there in my accustomed way I go through a series of dozens of steps, including the right choices of turns at street intersections. Yet I can "reel off" this program with the greatest of ease, hardly giving any attention to what comes next, much as I can put a cassette in a player, and it reels off a musical or other program.

One of the reasons humans have a huge brain is that we need and use a great number of programs to carry on our complex activities—thousands of times as many as the most intelligent of other animals. Exactly how that is achieved remains unknown, although the progress of researchers in the neurosciences suggests that we may have a good start toward understanding the neuronal, chemical, and molecular mechanisms involved within another few years.[4]

The Source of Programs

Present knowledge makes clear that programs can be acquired in two distinct ways: transmitted with the genes or learned after birth. As a general rule, the more brainpower an animal has, the more it learns after birth. The more neocortex or *new brain* it possesses, the greater the relative reliance on after-birth learning. We see once more why the laboratory rat and other small experimental animals can shed so little light on human learning: Their programs are largely species wisdom, transmitted genetically, while humans use the splendid new brain to do most learning after birth over many years.

No aspect of being human appears more dominant than this incessant accumulation of programs. The process, of course, is most rapid in the earlier years and then gradually tapers off. But since we live in a world that changes constantly, we are under far greater pressure than our forebears to continue to learn, to continue acquiring new programs. The man of 75 who is given a DVD player to honor that birthday must master some new programs to operate his new machine. A few centuries ago, the programs acquired by age 25 would pretty well see one through a full life; today much of what is learned by age 25 will become obsolete. Failure to keep on learning can prove restrictive, costly, or embarrassing.

How Programs Work

To carry on activities, one must constantly *select* a program from those that are stored in the brain and *implement* it—put it into use.[5] Even to walk across the room, one must use an extremely complex program involving many of the body's 600-plus muscles and the shifting of weight from one side to the other as the feet alternate in moving forward. The program has to be repeated every two paces, with continual fine adjustments to change direction or to pick up and carry articles. To walk, one program is used; to go up stairs, another; to go down stairs, a third. To take a stroll outside, one may have to use programs for going uphill, downhill, crossing rough ground, jumping over a puddle, or running a few steps to avoid traffic. *Each time, the program in use has to be switched off and another selected and switched on.* The brain does this so smoothly that we ordinarily are not aware of the switches being thrown, but this is the main key to our present insight into behavior.

When I am getting dressed in the morning and open a drawer full of shirts, I must make a conscious selection of which I will wear. After I have made that choice, opening up the shirt, putting it on, and buttoning it up "runs off" as a kind of automatic program to which I don't have to give any conscious attention unless something goes wrong—I find a button missing—and interferes.

Which shirt will I select? It depends on a perception of the *pattern* I will be dealing with. If I am going to a business meeting, I select a dress shirt; if I plan to make some repairs, I choose a work shirt; if I plan to exercise, I choose another type of shirt. Even more subtle patterns may influence me: I may want a conservative dress shirt for the meeting or a brighter one if the meeting will become a celebration with old friends. Though the decision may be trivial, I cannot act until some decision is made. (Following fixed habits or rituals, where possible, avoids decisions and so may seem more "comfortable.")

In much the same way, we select the most appropriate program from those stored in the brain to deal with what is happening at the time. For example, seeing stairs ahead, I select a going-up-stairs program. Having accidentally jostled somebody, I choose an offering-apology program. Facing an arithmetical problem, I tap my division program. Meeting a neighbor, I select a greeting program, complete with smile, nod, and suitable words.

THE PROGRAM IMPLEMENTATION CYCLE

In each of the above examples, a basic cycle is plainly in use. One must do the following:

1. *Evaluate* the situation or need (detect and identify the pattern or patterns being dealt with).

2. *Select* the most appropriate program from those stored.

3. *Implement* the program selected.

Human behavior looked at in these terms may hardly seem simple, but such a perspective provides more penetrating insight.

Key Observations

For educators, viewing behavior as a function of the program implementation cycle significantly expands our ability to observe and analyze student behavior during the learning process. Key observations include the following:

1. Unless the learner can reasonably and accurately evaluate the need or problem at hand (that is, detect and identify the patterns involved), the cycle goes astray at the outset. The student simply does not know what to do.

A familiar example is the student trying to cope with an arithmetic problem couched in words. Unable to detect the pertinent pattern, the student flounders, wondering whether to add, or divide, or give up entirely. Another example is the spelling of longer words. Lacking any sense of the structure or pattern of the word, the student tries to simply remember the order of the letters—perhaps producing some weird versions.[6]

2. People can access and use only those programs they already possess. However much one may be coerced or urged, or motivated or rewarded, there is no way to perform the program *unless it has already been stored.* He or she does not know how to do it. No program, no ability to perform the needed action.

There is no way to force a person to ride a bicycle, or play Chopin on the piano, or write a scientific paper, if those programs have not previously been acquired. That many other people can do these things has no bearing. Yet in almost any classroom, at any level, this principle is ignored. On the playground, one may hear a child being called "clumsy" or "poorly coordinated" when the real difficulty is that the child has not yet learned certain programs. In homes, parents scold children; in businesses, bosses scold employees—all in the same futile way for the same futile reason. *If the program has not been acquired, the solution is to acquire it,* not in criticizing, labeling, or giving a poor mark, practices that prove devastating to learners.

3. A student cannot implement a program unless given the chance to do so.

A test question might ask, "How can you verify the correct spelling of a word?" The answer intended is, "Look it up in a dictionary." A student who gives that answer, we must note, is not using that program. Rather, he or she is *using a program for answering a question on a test.* So commonly are tests used in instruction that this all-important difference may be overlooked; students may pass tests yet often be unable to carry out the programs themselves—a complaint loudly uttered today. Similarly, if students are always *directed* to use certain programs, there is no way to know whether they can detect the pattern, have a program to select, and can implement it. Rather, they are implementing programs *for following directions.* Such "learning" may prove fictitious.

As I indicated earlier, a program always has a goal, an objective—it is an activity to achieve some intended outcome. What happens if the program selected and implemented does not work?

When Programs Don't Work

During the program implementation cycle, the brain asks, "What *pattern* am I dealing with; what *program* should I choose to deal with it?" The most appropriate program is then implemented. Usually it will work. If it aborts, the brain must recycle—pattern detection, program selection, implementation. Let's say that I have taken out my keys to open the car door. I insert the key but it won't turn—the program *aborts.*

I must now go through the three-step cycle again: reevaluate the situation, select another program that seems appropriate, and implement that. Perhaps I have the wrong key, in which case I recycle to find the right one and try again. Perhaps the lock has jammed, so I recycle to the unusual program of going around to the opposite door.

Aborting Programs Is Disturbing

Aborting a program *always causes some degree of emotional shift* because the failure of a program to work is in general disturbing and *threatening,* especially when no workable alternative program can be found. The degree to which programs usually work when implemented to achieve the intended goal serves as a direct, continuous measure of how well one has "made sense of the world," how competent we generally are. Programs *should* work. When they do, confidence in oneself increases; when too often they don't, confidence diminishes.[7]

Impact on Self-Confidence. Teachers have long sensed that self-image and the belief that one can successfully learn is important to self-concept and, in turn, to learning. Brain research now concurs. An individual's confidence rises or falls when programs do or do not work. We can see too that children whose parents or teachers have over-directed their activities and over-stressed second-person estimates of achievement, may mistrust their own ability to evaluate situations and select appropriate programs.[8]

This program view of behavior, I submit, is consistent both with present scientific understandings of the brain and with what we can clearly see—once we know where to look—in the normal functioning of children, other adults, and ourselves. True, we cannot see into another person's brain to observe what pattern-detecting abilities and programs have been established there. However, we can see with new insights what happens when that person is allowed to use what he or she considers the most appropriate program—or when the individual has none to apply or can't identify the pertinent pattern to begin with.

ACQUISITION OF USEFUL PROGRAMS

The word *useful* in "acquisition of useful programs" deserves attention. Primarily, it means useful to the individual who will possess the program—in that person's view, rather than in someone else's view or to satisfy some supposed social or other standard. While it is true that one can be coerced into acquiring a program and may use it under duress, such programs are likely to become unused as soon as the duress ceases if good mental health prevails. If use of the forced program does continue, it usually will signify either superstitious ritual, with anxiety that something dreadful will occur if it is not used, or the inappropriate behavior that goes under the common name of neurosis. *Inherently, the use of a freely learned program satisfies; that of a coerced program brings back the old fears under which it was built.* We see this in mild form when people do arithmetic with obvious pain and reluctance and, in more serious degree, when individuals who have been forced to learn a musical instrument well cannot bear to play before an audience in later life.

Transfer of Learning

In a far wider sense, *useful* conveys the possibilities of *transfer* of learning, which can greatly increase the speed of new learning. For example, a program for roller skating can readily transfer to ice skating; one for using a typewriter keyboard can easily be extended to using a computer keyboard, which then can serve as a mental anchor for learning new information about the computer. *The ability to transfer some of these behavioral building blocks, adapting and adjusting them to new needs, explains why some individuals can master a new task far more rapidly than others* who lack the programs to transfer, or who in some cases may not yet have recognized the similarity of pattern involved which leads to and permits transfer.

Source of Creativity

The capacity to use old programs in fresh combinations seems to underlie what we call creativity. Greater sensitivity to pattern similarities facilitates the transfer. While I would doubt that sensitivity can be directly taught, it seems probable that it can be facilitated.

THE POWER OF PROGRAMS

The implications for education of the program concept of behavior—*evaluate, select, implement* program cycle—are stupendous, bringing not only fresh insights into human behavior but also generating some major guidelines for improving learning achievement.
The following is a summary:

1. We live by programs, switching on one after another, selecting from those that have been acquired and stored in the brain.

2. As humans, we are far more dependent on programs acquired by the tens of thousands after birth; in contrast, animals rely more on programs genetically transmitted.

3. A program is a fixed sequence for accomplishing some end—a goal, objective, or outcome. Our human nature makes the working of a program pleasurable; the concept of some after-the-event "reward" is neither necessary nor valid. However, feedback is essential to establish that the program did work more or less as intended.

4. We can use only those programs that have already been built and stored. What programs another person has, or many people have, has no bearing. If a person does not possess a program, efforts to force its use are absurd.

5. We routinely use a three-step cycle: evaluate the situation (involving pattern detection and recognition), select the program that seems most appropriate from our store, and implement it.

6. The abortion of a program—upon its failure to work—calls for recycling. When a high proportion of self-selected programs work well, confidence rises; when too many programs are aborted, confidence is reduced, and the learner may become far less able to self-select programs.

7. Although laboriously built, fully acquired programs have an automatic quality that can easily lead one to forget that other individuals may not have acquired these programs.

8. Learning can be defined as the acquisition of useful programs.

9. Learning progress can be properly evaluated only by observing *undirected* behavior.[9] Questioning and testing dealing primarily with *information* can reveal little. It shows only poorly what individuals can *do*.

10. Effective transfer of learning depends on using established programs in new applications and combinations. (Skill in putting together new combinations may equal "creativity.") The learner who can adapt established programs to new tasks by seeing similarities of patterns involved learns much more rapidly than one who cannot.

11. In general, if we regard human learning and behavior in terms of continually asking, "What program is being used?" sharp new insights can be gained and many confusions and misunderstandings avoided.

When extracting patterns and building programs, specific information may be helpful to the task or even required. But this does not imply that there is necessarily any great virtue in "stuffing the head with facts."

It can be handy to carry in memory certain information that will be frequently used. For example, we may store the phone numbers of a dozen people we often contact so we don't have to look them up each time. If patterns are involved, such information is much more easily remembered as when one knows that Tim, Linda, and Vance all work in the same office and can be reached through its main number at hours when that office will be open.

In our real world today, there exists vastly more information than can be memorized, and it tends to change or become obsolete rapidly, so that trusting memory can be treacherous.

A better strategy than trying to collect facts is to possess programs for finding various information—knowing what reference books are available and how to use them or where to obtain help. But until specific information is linked to need for pattern or program, it serves little purpose. When such needs exist, learners typically "gobble up" information at an astonishing rate because they see it has immediate and meaningful application.

More About Step Two of Learning—Developing Useful Programs

For further study, see the following:

- *Human Brain and Human Learning,* 3rd ed. (2002) by Leslie A. Hart, especially Chapters 9 and 10.
- *Exceeding Expectations: A User's Guide to Implementing Brain Research in the Classroom,* 4th ed. (2009), especially Chapter 5 (vol. 1).
- *Closing the Achievement Gap: Using the Environment as an Integrating Context for Learning* (1998), Executive Summary by Gerald A. Lieberman and Linda L. Hoody.

ENDNOTES

1. Leslie A. Hart, *Human Brain and Human Learning,* 3rd ed. (Black Diamond, WA: Books for Educators, 2002), 117, 139.

2. Hart, 350.

3. Hart, 145 and 165.

4. Recent research suggests that memory storage is not restricted only to the brain but is a bodybrain function (see Chapter 5). However, until researchers can provide a clear, detailed picture of how this functions, we will continue to refer to the brain as the location for storing programs.

5. This is true be it in academics, behavior, or motor skills.

6. Leslie A. Hart talked with James Doran, director of Algonquin Reading Camp, Rhinelander, Wisconsin, who demonstrated a simple, quick technique for giving students a sense of pattern that produces startling gains in their competency in spelling. Doran's brain-compatible methods also produced large, rapid gains in reading.

    For truly surprising gains in reading, see the Auditory Discrimination in Depth Program (ADD) and Visualizing and Verbalizing for Improved Comprehension by Lindamood-Bell. For information, contact the Lindamood-Bell Reading Processes Center, San Luis Obispo, California, 1-800-233-8756.

7. Self-esteem or self-concept programs have long had a questionable base, primarily a "touchy-feely" approach aimed at "feeling good about yourself" as a result of others' telling you that you are a "good person" (sometimes in the face of evidence to the contrary). Current brain research tells a different story about the brain's producing and receiving its own opiate-like molecules as a response to mental programs that work, to a sense of competence in handling the world. See Candace Pert, Ph.D., *Molecules of Emotion: Why You Feel the Way You Feel* (New York: Scribner, 1997); Stanley I. Greenspan, M.D., with Beryl Lieff Benderly, *The Growth of the Mind and the Endangered Origins of Intelligence* (New York: Addison-Wesley Publishing Company, 1997), 104; and Robert Sylwester, "The Neurobiology of Self-Esteem and Aggression," *Educational Leadership,* 54 (February 1997), 75–78.

8. Parents might well ask if this over-emphasis on valuing of performance by a second person might not also contribute to the extraordinary power of peer groups and peer pressure during the teen years (and beyond). See Alfie Kohn, *Punished by Rewards: The Trouble With Gold Stars, Incentive Plans, A's, Praise, and Other Bribes* (Boston: Houghton Mifflin, 1993) and *Beyond Discipline: From Compliance to Community* (Alexandria, VA: ASCD, 1996).

9. Teachers "driving" a conventional class and initiating most activity have little chance to observe what students do on their own. In good "open" classroom environments, Montessori, or similar settings, teachers can readily become observers because they have time and can be more detached. Students feel relaxed and absorbed in their work rather than on guard against criticism or a bad mark.

Appendix C—Age Appropriateness

A young child's brain is not a junior version of an adult brain with less information in it. It processes differently. The human brain unfolds in predictable developmental stages. Each stage is like an ever more complex template laid over the top of the previous one. At each of these stages, the brain is capable of more complex thinking, comparing, and analyzing.

Following is a brief overview of developmental stages based on Dr. Larry Lowery's application of Piaget's work[1] to science education. It is taken from Dr. Lowery's presentations to administrators and teachers of the Mid-California Science Improvement Program (MCSIP, 1987–1997) and from his book, *Thinking and Learning: Matching Developmental Stages With Curriculum and Instruction.*[2]

As you read through these pages, it's important to note that although the age at which each capacity comes into place is accurate for most students, there will be some students who reach a developmental stage earlier, and some will reach it later. For the late arrivals, if the mental scaffolding doesn't exist for learning a particular concept, they will need much more full sensory, *being there* experiences. A slower developmental timetable is usually due to fewer relevant, full-sensory experiences.

Another important lesson is that just because some students can understand something doesn't mean that all students at that age can. Science content is too often selected on the basis of what a few precocious students are capable of understanding, not what all students are developmentally capable of.

AGE THREE TO FIRST GRADE: COMPARING THE KNOWN TO THE UNKNOWN

During this stage of life, children learn to understand more words (and the concepts behind them) than they will for the rest of their lives. The child does this by putting real, concrete objects through what is called one-to-one correspondences—putting two objects together on the basis of a single property and learning from these comparisons more than was known before. According to Lowery, the child constructs fundamental concepts about the physical world and its properties (similarity and difference comparisons by size, shape, color, texture, etc.), about ordinal and cardinal numbers (one-to-one correspondence of varying degrees), about all measures (comparison of known to unknown), and about the use of symbols to stand for meaning (word recognitions).[3]

The major mode of operation at this stage is trial and error. Often, adults mistakenly try to help the child in an attempt to reduce or eliminate error, or they reprimand the child for making an error. This is unfortunate because children, like scientists, learn as much (sometimes more) from errors as from expected, correct results. Whether putting puzzle shapes into the wrong space, putting shoes on the wrong feet while learning to dress, or falling off a tricycle, for the child, an error spurs the learning process along.

An important characteristic of this stage is that the child does not yet have the ability to group objects using more than one property simultaneously,[4] such as pairings based on size, color, shape, texture, or speed. The three- to six-year-old may also arrange objects by chaining, that is, the third object in the chain shares an important characteristic with the second object (which was initially chosen to pair with the first object) based on a different characteristic.

This stage is variously described as the ability to put two objects together on the basis of a single property[5] or learning by one-to-one correspondence. Piaget calls it the *pre-operational stage.*

According to Larry Lowery, educators, because they have not considered the relationships between knowledge of the learner, instruction, and subject matter, "have seldom provided experiences that allow the potential of this stage to develop."[6] As a result, "curriculum materials water down advanced concepts. The cognitive demands of these tasks are often beyond the youngster's level."[7] In contrast, "when teachers challenge children to use this stage of thinking ability, the challenge usually takes the form of a rote-memory or recall routine, something the youngsters can do—but they can do so much more! Unfortunately for the development of students' thinking, teachers predominantly teach the rote-memory or recall routine throughout all the school years."[8]

The scientific thinking processes appropriate for this developmental level are observing, communicating, and comparing two items using just one property at a time. At this developmental level, the emphasis should be on exploration, wide-ranging experiences with the real world, sometimes referred to as "messing around" with real things in the real world. Context is important.

The following are age-appropriate main science ideas recommended by grade level:

For kindergarten—People can learn about things around them by observing them carefully—what they are made of, how they are put together, what they do, and how they are similar and different. Observing and comparing similarities and differences is a key way to help interpret and understand our world. Often, we can learn even more about those things if we do something to them and note what happens.[9]

For first grade—All living things, including humans, have basic needs (food; water; air; protection from weather, disease, and predators; and reproduction). A habitat is the place where the animal or plant lives while meeting these needs.[10]

SECOND TO THIRD GRADE: PUTTING THINGS TOGETHER, TAKING THINGS APART

At this stage, a child develops the capability to group all objects in a set on the basis of one common attribute (as compared to putting only two objects together on the basis of a single property). This capacity begins at about age six (usually late in the sixth year) and is established for most youngsters by age eight.

According to Lowery, "for the first time the student's mental construct is comprehensive and has a rationale or logic to it. . . . Simple rules can be understood and generated by the student if given the opportunity."[11]

At this stage, students do less trial and error exploration and are more thoughtful about the actions they impose upon their environment; they create an internal mental structure of those manipulations.[12] An important aspect of students' actions is the rearrangement of the materials with which they work. Students also have the capacity to do things in reverse direction without distorting the concept, for example, $3 + 2 = 5$ and $5 - 2 = 3$. This is one of the powerful aspects of thinking at this stage.[13]

From an adult's perspective, there is a correct and an incorrect way to put things together or take them apart; the child at variance is thus seen as having done the job incorrectly. Rather than just judging the task, however, adults should also examine the reason why the student chose that particular response and then focus on what the answers reveal about the accuracy and depth of the student's understanding.

To understand that numbers or ideas may be combined in any order, yet it is possible to return without distorting to the starting place, is a really big deal for students in second and third grade.

According to Larry Lowery, "the ability of the mind to do this—reverse direction without distorting the concept—is one of the powerful aspects of thinking at this stage. And the ability to think in this manner separates humans from computers (which cannot solve problems beyond a binary, comparing solution) and other primates (chimps, baboons, and orangutans can solve problems at the comparing stage but not at this stage)."[14]

This stage is variously described as the ability to put all objects together on the basis of a consistent, single property rationale or putting things together and returning things to the way they were.[15] Piaget's term is *early concrete operations*.

The scientific thinking processes appropriate for this developmental level are observing, communicating, and comparing, but at this developmental stage, using two or more properties at a time. At this developmental level, content should become more conceptual, that is, study of big ideas that form a web that captures many related ideas. While exploration and wide-ranging experiences with the real world remain essential for high levels of sensory input, less concrete ideas can be explored.

The following are age-appropriate main science ideas recommended by grade level:

For second grade—The physical characteristics of animals and plants vary greatly and determine what they can do and how they do it in order to meet their needs. Similarly, the physical characteristics of nonliving things vary greatly and determine what changes can occur in them and how they can be used.[16]

For third grade—Things are changing around us all the time. Change can occur in a variety of ways (reversible, irreversible; controllable, not controllable; steady or repetitive and thus fairly predictable or not and thus unpredictable) and for different reasons. The rate and size of change may not be observable with human senses; tools to measure such change are needed. Change can be helpful, harmful, or neutral.[17]

FOURTH TO SIXTH GRADE: SIMULTANEOUS IDEAS

At about ages eight to ten, children develop the capacity to mentally coordinate two or more properties or concepts at a time. According to Lowery, when this capacity is in place—which may occur as early as age eight or as late as age ten—students can comprehend place value in math, the need for controlling variables in a science experiment, and the use of similes and multiple themes in literature, and can begin to conceptualize the common intersection of more than one idea and can comprehend the logic that results, such as, in social studies, the relationships that exist in free trade.[18] According to Lowery, "as with earlier capabilities, this new one integrates with those preceding it much like a new map of greater abstraction that can be overlaid upon other layers of maps."[19]

At this stage, students enjoy puns and can easily learn about homonyms. In their writing, they shift to using multiple descriptors: "an old, bent, tired man." They shift from trial-and-error thinking to contemplating the effects of comparing two or more things under different situations.[20] Arrangement of objects now indicates the intersection of multiple properties.

However, students at this developmental level are not yet ready to handle the traditional science "experiment" of stating a hypothesis, controlling the variables, and conducting the systematic testing of each variable individually while all others are held constant in order to determine which are relevant and which have no effect. Unfortunately, our traditional school curriculum treats elementary students as young adults. Yet for our young adults—high school students—the curriculum for the non-college bound is a rerun of what students were given in elementary school and thus is unchallenging and often boring.

Piaget refers to this stage as *late concrete operations;* Lowery's term is *simultaneity of ideas.*[21]

The scientific thinking processes appropriate for this developmental level are observing, communicating, comparing, and organizing. At this developmental level, content should be based in concepts that in turn are based in *being there* experiences. Note that, although students at this level can understand the need for controlling variables in science,[22] it is not until high school that students' cognitive maps allow them to successfully process the typical science experiment with its multiple variables.

The following are age-appropriate main science ideas recommended by grade level:

For fourth grade—Plants and animals interact with each other and their environment in ways that allow them to meet their basic needs. Keep in mind that humans are animals.[23]

For fifth grade—All structures and systems, living and nonliving, are made up of smaller parts and/or processes.[24]

For sixth grade—Both living and nonliving systems have situations in which they change in some way and other situations in which they remain essentially unchanged or constant. Why situations in such systems change and why they remain constant can be explained in terms of particular variables. Much change in our world is human made; some is intended and some inadvertent.[25]

The idea of age appropriateness is certainly not new. Montessori, Piaget, and Vygotsky have addressed the issue quite clearly. Yet it just gets pushed aside by tradition and politics when textbooks and state frameworks are being created. A glance through textbooks from the past several decades shows tradition at its most mindless and blind adherence to "the way we've always done it."

ENDNOTES

1. The pioneering work on the growth of intelligence was done by Swiss psychologist Jean Piaget (1896–1980), one of the most significant psychologists of the twentieth century. Since Piaget, others have studied these developmental stages, including Erickson (1950), Bruner (1966), Gagne (1970), and Vygotsky (1974–1997). Larry Lowery, formerly with the Lawrence Hall of Science and

instructor at the University of California, Berkeley, provides one of the most practical explanations of developmental levels for those engaged in curriculum development. Because Lowery applies growth of intelligence specifically to science curriculum and instruction, we have chosen to use his point of view. See Lawrence Lowery, *Thinking and Learning: Matching Developmental Stages With Curriculum and Instruction* (Black Diamond, WA: Books for Educators, 1996), 2.

Also see "Two Important Ideas About Thinking From Vygotsky" (www.tsg .suny.downloadfiles/vcresources/Two Important Ideas about Thinking from Vygotsky). Vygotsky's term for age appropriateness is *zone of proximal development* (ZPD)—the range of tasks that are too difficult for the child to master alone but that can be learned with guidance and assistance of adults or more skilled students. The lower limit of the ZPD is the level of skill reached by the child working independently. The upper limit is the level of additional responsibility the child can accept with the assistance of an able instructor. When a child cannot understand something with assistance, Lowery calls such content age inappropriate. Failing to understand, students must resort to memorization which is often experienced as frustrating and boring.

Vygotsky's pivotal work, *Thought and Language,* was written in 1934 and is still used in child development classes at universities and colleges throughout the United States.

2. Larry Lowery's *Thinking and Learning: Matching Developmental Stages With Curriculum and Instruction* is a gem of a book and a "must read" for all who work on curriculum. It's the only book I know that provides a realistic and understandable look at what students can understand versus what must be memorized.

3. Lowery, 17–19.

4. Lowery, 21.

5. Lowery, 19.

6. Lowery, 22.

7. Lowery, 22.

8. Lowery, 22.

9. Karen D. Olsen, *Science Continuum of Concepts, K–6* (Black Diamond, WA: Books for Educators, 2009), 6.

10. Olsen, 12.

11. Lowery, *Thinking and Learning,* 33.

12. Lowery, 35.

13. Lowery, 36.

14. Lowery, 36.

15. Lowery, 34.

16. Olsen, *Science Continuum of Concepts, K–6,* 20.

17. Olsen, 27.

18. Lowery, *Thinking and Learning,* 43.

19. Lowery, 39.

20. Lowery, 40.

21. Lowery, 42.

22. Lowery, 43, 75, 77–78.

23. Olsen, *Science Continuum of Concepts, K–6,* 32.

24. Olsen, 38.

25. Olsen, 44.

Glossary

***Being There* Experiences**—opportunities to experience a concept or skill in a real-world context so that what it is (the pattern) and how to use it (the program) are directly experienced through all 19 senses. These opportunities also provide increased emotional involvement (see Chapter 9) and movement (see Chapter 8). Allowing students to watch experts do their thing activates their mirror neurons, the neurons used for learning through mimicry. The power of this is obvious in young children. It has been prescribed for learners of all ages by John Dewey and others as "learning by doing." The current brain research in this area is powerful and conclusive.

Double-Link Curriculum—a model for developing curriculum to ensure that teachers have the content they need to teach through both steps of learning, to mastery of application of concepts and skills and their wiring into long-term memory. The Integrated Thematic Instruction model (ITI), now known as *Highly Effective Teaching* (*HET*), calls these two links key points and inquiries.

Effective First Teaching—an expectation that teaching something the first time should be effective—from introduction to the ability to apply, to wiring into long-term memory—thereby eliminating the need for repetition and remediation.

Game Plan Scenarios—an outline of how to use this book when facing three different timelines and levels of preparedness for budget cutting (pages 1.9–1.11).

HET—*Highly Effective Teaching*, a model for implementing what we know about how the brain learns; a comprehensive model for curriculum development and selection of instructional strategies. Formerly known as the Kovalik ITI (Integrated Thematic Instruction) model.

Immersion Input—replicates the real-world context of the *being there* experience used to anchor current study. It involves transforming a classroom into a living model of the *being there* location, containing as much hands-on-of-the-real-thing items as possible. For example, if a pond is the *being there* experience, the classroom would have a small pond (child's swimming pool) with as many real pond critters and plants as possible. The room itself would look like a pond—blue film over the windows to simulate the water line; replicas of plants and animals at, above, and below the water line on the walls; at least 50 resources—books, other printed materials, multimedia, and, of course, Internet access to relevant information; a CD playing pond sounds; models and pictures of pond animals and plants available for close study and exploration; and Internet access.

Inseparable Bodybrain Partnership—Current brain research indicates that the limbic system is part of a larger emotional system involving "information substances" produced and received throughout the body as well as in the brain. In other words, the brain talks to the body, and the body talks back to the brain. Also, the body, through aerobic exercise, directly promotes and enhances brain function. Learning is thus the result of an inseparable bodybrain partnership.

Neurogenesis—the process of neurons dividing and propagating; neurons are born as blank-slate stem cells; the process is spurred by several factors—IGF-1 (insulin-like growth factor), VEGF (vascular endothelial growth factor), FGF-2 (fibroblast growth factor)—which, during exercise, push through the blood-brain barrier and interact with BDNF (brain-derived neurotrophic factor). This cocktail accelerates learning. This occurs primarily in the hippocampus and requires a development process in which the cells find something to do (learn) or they die.

19 Senses—Exactly how many senses we humans possess is still an open question. Some sources cite as many as 22 but certainly more than the traditional five.

PE4Life—An approach developed by Napperville High School, Chicago, to implementing what's known from brain research about the relationship between aerobic exercise and learning.

Strategy-Builder Chart—a chart that ranks the program areas addressed in this book according to the following: (a) the potential for money that can be cut ("Source of Money to Cut") and (b) where high achievement increases can be had at low cost ("Cost-Efficiency Ratio—High Achievement Increase for Low Cost"), page 1.5.

Two-Step Learning—a definition of learning based on Leslie A. Hart's model of learning as a pattern seeking and program building process.

List of Figures

L.2 What Brain Research Can Teach About Cutting School Budgets

About the Author

Karen D. Olsen (B.S., M.A., M.Ed.) brings a wealth of experience to her writing. The product of learning in a one-room school for grades 1 to 8 and growing up on a ranch, Karen has forever retained her insistence that what we learn should be usable in very practical as well as academically rigorous ways. Following doctoral studies at Columbia University Teachers College, she worked for the California State Department of Education for 12 years. Her assignments included planning and development—writing schoolwide planning and quality program review documents and processes—and management of the school consortium unit serving districts highly committed to school change.

Karen was one of the original founders of the California Institute of School Improvement, a nonprofit foundation designed to support schools and districts in a wide range of school change issues. As program director, she conducted seminars ranging from implications of recent legislation to schoolwide planning and quality review processes, to the role of change agent for mentor teachers. During this time, she wrote an insightful mentor book, *California Mentor Teacher Role: Owner's Manual,* which grew out of her experiences working with more than 7,000 mentor teachers throughout the state.

Ms. Olsen was the Executive Director of the Mid-California Science Improvement Program, a 10-year effort funded by the David and Lucile Packard Foundation to improve the quality of science education based on the ITI model (now referred to as *HET—Highly Effective Teaching*). She wrote *Kid's Eye View of Science: A Teacher's Handbook for Implementing an Integrated Thematic Approach to Science, K–6* (coauthored with Susan Kovalik), *Classroom Stages of Implementation, Coaching for the HET/ITI Model: Delivering on the Promise,* and *Science Continuum of Concepts, K–6* to support that effort. Karen also served as Executive Director of the Bay Area

Middle School Program, a project to create model middle schools, also funded by the Packard Foundation.

Karen coauthored, with Susan Kovalik, *ITI: The Model* and *Exceeding Expectations: User's Guide for Implementing Brain Research in the Classroom.* She is also author, coauthor, or contributing editor of the following ITI/HET books: *The Way We Were, The Way We Can Be: A Vision for the Middle School; Synergy, The Transformation of America's High Schools; Schoolwide Stages of Implementation;* and *Tools for Citizenship and Life: Implementing the ITI/HET Lifelong Guidelines and LIFESKILLS in the Classroom.* Karen also updated *Human Brain and Human Learning* by Leslie A. Hart.

References

Blanchard, Ken and Margaret McBride. *The One-Minute Apology: A Powerful Way to Make Things Better.* (New York: William Morrow, 2003).

Brady, Marion. "No Dog Left Behind," *Education Week,* (January 28, 2009).

Brain Connection. (2009). http://www.brainconnection.com (accessed June 30, 2009).

Bruer, John T. "Education and the Brain: A Bridge Too Far," *Educational Researcher* 26, (November 1997): 4–16.

Cohen, Elizabeth. *Designing Groupwork: Strategies for the Heterogeneous Classroom,* 2nd ed. (New York: Teachers College Press, 1994).

Cohen, Isabel and Marcelle Goldsmith. *Hands On: How to Use Brain Gym in the Classroom: A Practical Photo Manual for Educators, Parents, and Learners.* (Ventura, CA: Edu-Kinesthetics, Inc., 2003).

Diamond, Marian and Janet Hopson. *Magic Trees of the Mind: How to Nurture Your Child's Intelligence, Creativity, and Healthy Emotions From Birth Through Adolescence.* (New York: Penguin, 1998).

Gardner, Howard. *Frames of Mind: Theory of Multiple Intelligences,* 10th ed. (New York: Perseus Books Group, 1993).

Gibbs, Jeanne. *Reaching All by Creating TRIBES Learning Communities.* (Windsor, CA: CenterSource Systems, 2006).

Goerner, Sally. *The Coming Great Change in Education: A Practical Guide to How Scientific and Social Movements Are Remaking Our World and Our Schools.* (Black Diamond, WA: Books for Educators, 2006).

Goldberg, Elkhonon. *The Executive Brain: Frontal Lobes and the Civilized Mind.* (Oxford: Oxford University Press, 2001).

Goldberg, Elkhonon. *The New Executive Brain: Frontal Lobes and the Civilized Mind.* (New York: Oxford University Press, 2009).

Gossen, Diane and Judy Anderson. *Creating the Conditions: Leadership for Quality Schools.* (Chapel Hill, NC: New View Publications, 1995).

Hart, Leslie A. *How the Brain Works: A New Understanding of Human Learning, Emotion, and Thinking.* (New York: Basic Books, 1975).

Hart, Leslie A. *Human Brain and Human Learning,* 3rd ed. (Black Diamond, WA: Books for Educators, 2002).

Hawkins, Jeff with Sandra Blakeslee. *On Intelligence: How a New Understanding of the Brain Will Lead to the Creation of Truly Intelligent Machines.* (New York: Times Books/Henry Holt and Company, 2004).

Healy, Jane. *Endangered Minds: Why Children Don't Think—and What We Can Do About It.* (New York: Simon & Schuster, 1990).

Katz, Michael B. *Class, Bureaucracy, & Schools: The Illusion of Educational Change in America.* (New York: Praeger Publishers, 1971).

Kaufelt, Martha Miller. *I Can Divide and Conquer: A Concept in a Day* (DVD). (Federal Way, WA: Susan Kovalik & Associates, 1987).

Kennedy, Robert. *Kids Say the Darndest Things!* http://privateschool.about .com/od/humor/qt/darndest.htm (accessed June 30, 2009).

Kohn, Alfie. *Punished by Rewards: The Trouble With Gold Stars, Incentive Plans, A's, Praise, and Other Bribes.* (Boston: Houghton Mifflin, 1993).

Kohn, Alfie. "Rethinking Homework," *Principal,* (January/February, 2007).

Kohn, Alfie. "Test Today, Privatize Tomorrow: Using Accountability to 'Reform' Public Schools to Death," *Phi Delta Kappan,* (April, 2004).

Kohn, Alfie. *The Homework Myth: Why Our Kids Get Too Much of a Bad Thing.* (New York: Da Capo Press, 2006).

Kovalik, Susan J. and Karen D. Olsen. *Exceeding Expectations: A User's Guide to Implementing Brain Research in the Classroom,* 4th ed. (Federal Way, WA: The Center for Effective Learning, 2009).

Lieberman, Gerald A. and Linda L. Hoody. *Closing the Achievement Gap: Using the Environment as an Integrating Context for Learning,* Executive Summary. (San Diego, CA: State Education and Environment Roundtable, 1998).

Lowery, Lawrence F. *Thinking and Learning: Matching Developmental Stages With Curriculum and Instruction.* (Black Diamond, WA: Books for Educators, 1995).

Medina, John. *Brain Rules: 12 Principles for Surviving and Thriving at Work, Home, and School.* (Seattle, WA: Pear Press, 2008).

Miller, Norma, ed. *The Healthy School Handbook: Conquering the Sick Building Syndrome and Other Environmental Hazards in and Around Your School.* (Washington, DC: NEA Professional Library, 1995).

Mission Addition: A Concept in Three Days (DVD). (Federal Way, WA: Susan Kovalik & Associates, 2003).

Olsen, Karen D. *Coaching for the HET/ITI Model: Delivering on the Promise.* (Black Diamond, WA: Books for Educators, 2009).

Olsen, Karen D. *Science Continuum of Concepts, K–6.* (Black Diamond, WA: Books for Educators, 2009).

Pearson, Sarah S. *Finding Common Ground: Service Learning and Education Reform.* (Washington, D.C.: American Youth Policy Forum, 2002).

Pert, Candace. *Molecules of Emotion: Why You Feel the Way You Feel.* (New York: Scribner, 1997).

Probell, Johah. *Brain Teasers.* (2007). http://jonahprobell.com/brainteasers.html (accessed June 30, 2009).

Ratey, John J. with Eric Hagerman. *Spark: The Revolutionary New Science of Exercise and the Brain.* (New York: Little, Brown and Company, 2008).

Ratey, John J. *A User's Guide to the Brain: Perception, Attention, and the Four Theaters of the Brain.* (New York: Pantheon Books, 2001).

Reigeluth, Charles M., Ph.D. *Instructional-Design Theories and Models, vol. 2: A New Paradigm of Instructional Theory.* (London: Lawrence Erlbaum Associates, Publishers, 1999).

Smith, Frank. *Insult to Intelligence: The Bureaucratic Invasion of Our Classrooms.* (New York: Arbor House, 1986).

Sylwester, Robert. *How to Explain a Brain: An Educator's Handbook of Brain Terms and Cognitive Processes.* (Thousand Oaks, CA: Corwin, 2005).

Sylwester, Robert. *The Adolescent Brain: Reaching for Autonomy.* (Thousand Oaks, CA: Corwin, 2007).

Tuckman, Bruce. *The Teambuilding Company,* www.teambuilding.co.uk/ (accessed August 22, 2009).

Wei, R. C., L. Darling-Hammond, A. Andree, N. Richardson, and S. Orphanos, "Professional Learning in the Learning Professions: A Status Report on Teacher Development in the United States and Abroad," *National Staff Development Council* (February, 2009). Also available at http://www.ecs.org/00CN4246.

.

Index

CORWIN
A SAGE Company

The Corwin logo—a raven striding across an open book—represents the union of courage and learning. Corwin is committed to improving education for all learners by publishing books and other professional development resources for those serving the field of PreK–12 education. By providing practical, hands-on materials, Corwin continues to carry out the promise of its motto: **"Helping Educators Do Their Work Better."**